EVOLUTIONARY

TALES

FROM

DR. YES!

Part 3
"The YES! Trilogy"

EVOLUTIONARY TALES

from

DR. YES!

**A prescription of contemporary stories
for Affirmative Living**

Allan C. Somersall Ph.D., M.D.
Author of "A Passion For Living"

Evolutionary Tales Of Dr. YES!

Published By:
ProMotion Publishing
3368F Governor Drive
San Diego, CA 92122

(800) 231-1776

ISBN 1-57901-022-9

Printed in the United States of America

Books by Dr. Allan C. Somersall:

Your Evolution to YES!
- 111 Steps to Affirmative Living

Understanding The Evolution of YES!
- Insights for Affirmative Living

Evolutionary Tales from Dr. YES!
- A prescription of contemporary stories for Affirmative Living

A Passion For Living
- The Art of Real Success

Your Very Good Health
- 101 Healthy Lifestyle Choices

To
my mother,
who first taught
me to say

YES!

ACKNOWLEDGEMENTS

The author is indebted to several people for their valuable contributions that have made this book a reality: To John McIlroy and Dorothy Pilarski-McIlroy for many valuable discussions and significant work on the preliminary drafting; to my wife Virginia, for her encouragement and support through long, tedious nights as well as her valued criticism and editing; to Tara Guptill for most incisive insights and editing; to my agent, Carolina Loren, for arduous typesetting and computer editing, as well as for championing the work and guiding it through to completion; to Sophie Shena for typing and retyping the manuscript; to Patti Shaffer for useful comments. Without such a strong supporting cast, this book would still be an intangible dream. Thanks to each and all of you for your contributions. In the end, all remaining shortcomings are mine.

PREFACE

*The **YES!** Trilogy: The Evolution of **YES!***

This is your world, its length and breadth, its height and depth. It's all yours to explore. You have the right to be here and the privilege to do almost anything and to go almost anywhere. Yes, you do. So fasten your seatbelt.

Imagine yourself ... with your smiling face bathed in rays of sunshine and the thrust of rocket engines propelling you on your first solo flight into the unknown. This is the inevitable challenge for you to meet if you are ever going to take control of your life or to realize your dream. No more excuses, no more hesitation, no more dependence or delay. You must decide. You must commit, you must let go. The countdown is over and now you're taking off.

Up, up and away!

Imagine the freedom, imagine the fun, but also imagine the apprehension and fear ... That's all okay. You're soon soaring high, high above the surrounding crowd who seem content to congratulate you and to cheer your success.

As you soar upward, defying the downward forces of negativity and indecision, your adrenals are pumping furiously. Your heart is racing and your nerves and muscles are strained to peak performance.

You scan the wide horizon of opportunity with the eye of an eagle. You can see clearly now. You are in control, alone. This is it. This is living as you dreamed it could be. What a thrill!

You choose to celebrate the exciting moment with both thumbs up and a deep, clear affirmation that compels you to shout out loudly and deliberately... **"y-y-YES!!!"**

But you may not have always been this way. Perhaps you once drifted in the shadows of doubt, defeat and despondency. You were losing hope. Then you experienced an evolution ... *The Evolution of* **YES!**

Come trace this evolutionary journey as you go through this book and discover the secrets of such a transformation. Come and enjoy the scenery and the sensations along the way, but make it a personal adventure. Get involved with the prospect and the process of change. Real personal change. It will be an exhilarating experience of growth, fulfillment and joy.

The **YES!** *Trilogy* was written to be very personal and to strike deep at the core personality where we are all prone to be defensive and protective. It was designed for you. The form and content of each page of each volume was elaborated with you in mind. It contains a message distilled and delivered to your heart's address that you must receive.

You will get back to basics as you probe the space in which you generally live and might even sometimes hide. But there is nothing to fear in the inevitable exposé. You will be encouraged all along the way. You will sense that you belong and that you can become whatever you aspire to be. It's a recurring theme.

That theme deserves a further word of explanation.

EVOLUTION

The *concept* of evolution is a very useful one. It allows us to arrange an array of data and of ideas, first in order of sequence, in time or space, and then in order of complexity, in value or importance. It provides a mental picture for convenient examination and reference. It adds perception, pattern and process to ideas. It gives form if not substance, and it explains effect if not cause.

For these reasons and more, we will exploit its pragmatic value as a *concept* throughout *The* **YES!** *Trilogy*.

The Evolution of **YES!** is about a progression and in the case of any particular individual, it may even define a process. It is *not* about the origin of any species. It is about you … your evolution. It is about your living today as an exclamation of all the positive, passionate and productive connotations implied by a strong, personal and affirmative **YES!**

It is about the origins of your personal style, the sources of your individual lifestyle and the way you choose to live your daily life. It is far more about practical psychology than about biology, with a spotlight on your attitudes and perspectives. It addresses your temperament and your degree of motivation.

These are critical variables. All such human characteristics are extremely important in determining the Life Equation: *What you put in equals what you get out.* It therefore addresses the real bottom line, yours included.

We will carefully trace a progression of responses to life that spans the extremes of **NO!** and **YES!** You will find a reflection of yourself somewhere along the continuum. That's guaranteed.

How do *you* now respond to life's challenges and opportunities?

- Are you prone to be negative? Do tend to you confess *"No, I can't"* before you even think?
- Do you feel left out, always looking on? When its show time, is it always *"somebody else but me"*?
- Do you insist *"I should ..."* but somehow, it seems you just can't go beyond that conviction?
- Will you only act *"If ...?"* That is, will your results

depend on all the right conditions being met?

- Perhaps you *"would really like to,"* but that is only daydreaming. Do you have real passion and clear focus?
- Do you keep adding *"But ..."* and just making excuses, one after another, both good and bad?
- Do you have really good intentions for *"one of these days"*, but you're forever putting things off?
- Sometimes you can hardly make a clear or firm decision. Did you say *"Perhaps"?* Just maybe?
- You really want to, but are you *"shy"*? Always slow and apologetic in response and always evading the spotlight?
- You say *"Yes"*, but are you content to just *"give it a try"?* Do you always have some reservation?
- Are you more committed than that, so that you will actually *"do your best"?* And is that ever enough?
- Will you respond with abandon? Will you affirm **YES!** and *"do it even if it kills you"?* There's a true **YES!**

Did you see a pattern? Did you recognize a progression? Could you even trace an *Evolution*?

However you characterize your response at this time, as you explore *The Evolution of* **YES!**, you will gain new insights that will inspire you to take affirmative action.

The new perspectives should then give you a better understanding of how and why you react to life's challenges and opportunities in the way that you do now. Then with practical suggestions and guidelines, you will be able to order your steps and keep moving. Eventually you will live out a superlative **YES!** Consistently so.

So follow each stage of development carefully.

YES!

Now, it is true that each of us would aspire and struggle to obtain a personal life characterized by positive thinking, buoyancy, passion, fulfillment and the like. Whatever your circumstances may be, you want to rise above them to experience, in principle, the best that is possible.

Health, wealth and the pursuit of happiness may not be truly your highest or strongest ideals. Presumably, you also want a life of affirmation, not apology. There's a big difference. So you want to express not just a right to be here but the rhyme, rhythm and reason for being here. Well, the poetry, music and logic of life coalesce in a single, explosive word that says it all ... **YES!**

Success is a three letter word ... **Y.E.S.!**

But what exactly does it mean?

This life of **YES!** will be described in detail as we progress through the evolving responses to life. And we cannot overstate the importance of the two *gigantic, little* words which form the bookends of this exploration: **NO!**

evolves to **YES!** as we traverse the grand dimensions of time, space and the human spirit.

All quality of life falls somewhere between these two polar extremes. It is a behavior pattern that we each adopt. Therefore, you can indeed characterize your own life even now by different stages or phases that dominate your responses to the challenges of today and every day. In this way, you define much of who you are and how you choose to live.

The Evolution of **YES!** will help you to put this all in context. You will come to appreciate that the quality of life you enjoy is largely yours to *choose*. It is a position that you take, it is a decision that you make. Your options can be as different as night and day.

On one extreme is the sad picture where one could experience life as a free fall in pessimism, negativism and defeat. This would be Phase One, a starting point. From this abyss, we will identify footholds or lifelines to hold on to. Then, from that dramatic beginning, we will trace an attitude to life that moves through progressive Phases towards affirmative and passionate living.

With vivid practical examples, we will consider common barriers to personal growth such as poor self-image, vicarious living, bad conscience, risk, wishful thinking, excuses, procrastination, indecision, shyness and more.

There will be a natural progression as each of these barriers is surmounted in turn. *The Evolution of* **YES!** will inspire you to rise above them all and to realize the best that you can possibly be. You will discover the life of **YES!**

The life of **YES!** represents the best that life has to offer. It defines a *possible mental attitude* that blends faith, optimism and assertiveness. More importantly, it defines a heart of *passion* that seeks to harness all the forces of imagination and the fire of human desire to become, to excel and to serve. It therefore defines also a life of *purpose and productivity*, a life that makes a difference and celebrates the joys of each moment as they connect into a pattern of growth and destiny.

TRILOGY

This trilogy of books began as a single volume, but the concept of **YES!** exploded in the author's mind as the gems of truth were mined. The continuum of change from **NO!** to **YES!** followed naturally along three orthogonal paths but retained a single pattern. It is a theme where fantasy, fact and fiction merge into a single three dimensional reality. That is essentially why *The* **YES!** *Trilogy* is synonymous with *The Evolution of* **YES!** It is three in one and yet one in three.

The heart of the message is clearly presented in Part 1, **Your Evolution to YES!**, where a compelling series of practical *Life Lines* is spelled out at each Phase. These *Life Lines* are all designed to help you get a grip on life and then keep moving along the course of evolution that consummates in Abandon. They are original, incisive and fascinating directives to follow. There you will discover the true life of **YES!** This is a perspective designed explicitly for the *pragmatic* mind. It is action oriented and you should aim to apply the *Life Lines* to advantage where appropriate.

In Part 2, **Understanding The Evolution of YES!**, there is a progressive series of insightful *Commentaries* to further elucidate, in each Phase, the issues and hurdles that one must overcome to get to **YES!** It explains why in psychological terms and how different responses to life's challenges and opportunities originate. But it goes beyond life's problems to identify solutions for affirmative living. This perspective is designed for the *probing* mind. You will want to construct your own analysis for sure. Try doing that.

In Part 3, **Evolutionary Tales from DR. YES!**, each Phase is illustrated by the portrait of a fictitious character in an original short story that will keep you guessing. This perspective is designed for the *pensive* mind. Each tale is more than just a tale. It is both a mirror and a makeover in poetry at the end. You should ponder the meaning and implications of each *Vignette* for your own life situation and response.

You will probably have a preference for one art form or the other. But the true or full content of this amazing metamorphosis will not be clearly seen until you grasp all three perspectives. So say **YES!** to all three parts.

You may begin reading the trilogy wherever you choose. A quick glance through the Table of Contents in each case will give you the guideposts which may identify for you a most convenient starting point. You could already know exactly where you have parked or met a roadblock in your response to life, and that would be a great place to get into the flow.

However, sooner or later you will want to cover the entire evolutionary path to **YES!** in the complete trilogy. Part 3 will pick you up on the earth, Part 2 will lead you to the horizon, and Part 1 will take you to the skies. From there you will shine like the star that you really are.

But you are admonished to take your time. Explore small areas at any one sitting so that you can discover all there is and apply the many practical suggestions. Read and re-read where necessary to internalize the precepts.

The **YES!** *Trilogy* is provocative yet practical, full of priceless quotes, interesting anecdotes and insightful social observations. The best principles of psychological theory are incorporated into a framework of self-reliance, with the motivation to live decisively and productively, while you remain controlled and relaxed.

After all, life proves to be truly exhilarating to those who, in any arena, learn to say a resounding **YES!** in the face of both challenge and opportunity. They are the ones who believe and commit to what they really want. They go for it with everything and they invariably find gold. So can you.

You must find the growing inspiration on every page, as picturesque illustrations will be woven into a beautiful mosaic of passion, truth and beauty. You will then emerge and finally affirm to live with conviction and enthusiasm, the exclamation of … **"y-y-YES!!!"**

As you continue to grow and mature, you will get closer to becoming:

one hundred percent *positive,*
one hundred percent *passionate,* and
one hundred percent *productive!*

YES! You can. **YES!** You must. **YES!** You will.

YES! YES!! YES!!!

Contents

In the beginning...

NO!

1

No Tropical Escape

("No, I can't")

When we think well of ourselves,
when we cause others to think well of us and
when we meet the standards we have set for ourselves,
we plant seeds of life in fertile ground for our self-esteem to grow.

—A.C.S.

In the northern corners of the world, freezing rain, drifting snow and gale force winds are not exactly meteorological novelties, especially during the short, dark days of February that never seem to end. It does get cold.

On this Tuesday morning, Gloria was grateful to be indoors at least. She sat at her stylish Steelcase workstation staring out and off into the gloom. For three days she had been fighting a lingering depression.

Maybe a coffee just now would do the trick. Gloria walked over to the kitchenette and took a mug off the hook. As she reached for the coffee pot, a colorful picture on the bulletin board caught her eye.

Tacked up on the cork were two postcards from Lucille Winston who was now finishing up her second week of a winter vacation at a popular Caribbean sunspot. Gloria's first instinct was to throw them into the trash can in frustration but instead, she took them back to her desk.

Like a small child totally transfixed, Gloria stared at the postcards. As she looked at them the sand got whiter, the sunshine brighter and the sky bluer. Why not get on the first plane heading south and let the sand, sun and surf heal her troubled spirit?

Oh ... the joy of a great idea!

Gloria opened her Rolodex and flipped through the cards until she got to T- Travel Agents. One question after another was racing through her mind. Money? Credit? Time? No problem. She even had vacation time coming to her. Maybe someone would decide to go with her, or maybe not. She would sort that out later. First, buy the tickets.

With a tinge of excitement, Gloria picked up the telephone and made the call.

"Hell-o-o ..."

An hour later, with a big grin plastered across her face, Gloria made another trip to the coffee machine, this time wiggling as she walked. She tacked the pictures back on the board, poured herself a coffee and suppressed an urge to giggle.

Her imagination was working overtime. It would be perfect. She would fly out on Thursday and spend ten days in the Caribbean. By the time she got back, the weather would have to be better. But even if it wasn't, she would be in better shape to handle it. Right!

Her anticipation was growing with time.

Late that afternoon, as she stood on the drafty platform waiting for her subway train, Gloria anticipated none of the irritation that she usually felt at being stuck with the masses, freezing her butt and then having to stand all the way home on the train. Today she was too busy leafing through the Fodor's Travel Guide she had picked up at the bookstore. Far from waning, her good mood steadily improved all day to the point where she was quite ebullient when the train pulled into the station.

Putting her book away, Gloria made her way to the back of the car and leaned against the railing. She dreamily thought of swaying palm trees, eighty degree weather, and white sandy beaches. So what if the trip would stretch her credit card limit to the maximum ...? She needed to get out of the cold, and the temperature was not even half the problem.

Anything else had to be better than this.

Weeks of cold, dark days filled with slush and ice were indeed only a tiny part of her misery. What about the lack of quality single men in this city? That was an obvious fact, she thought, to any woman over the age of eighteen. There she went again ... needing a relationship to define herself. Even at twenty-seven. How could she possibly have a meaningful relationship when everyone else around her seemed so busy and so cold? Gloria answered her own question out loud.

"Obviously ... *I can't.*"

And what about her career? How could she ever advance up the corporate ranks in a company that apparently placed merit near the bottom of its list of promotion criteria? And besides that, weren't they now eliminating most middle management jobs anyway? Look how long it had taken her to finally achieve the one little pathetic promotion after six long years on the job. Gloria again answered her thoughtful question out loud, but in a soft whisper.

"Right again, Holmes ... obviously, *I can't.*"

Gloria reluctantly checked off the items on her emerging mental list: her frustrated love life, her boring job, her limited career prospects, her neglected family, her shallow social life, and her negative financial situation. The same type of questions yielded the same type of answers.

"I wish I could do something about the mess I seem to be in.. But ... *No, I can't.*"

The irony of Gloria's situation was that the people around her - her parents, her friends, her work mates, her neighbors - all thought that Gloria had life by the tail. They perceived that she had a good job and a beautiful apartment in a trendy suburban complex. She drove a late model sports convertible and was a popular cheerleader among the yuppies who frequented the uptown cafés. She was a young college graduate in good health, with a reputation as the life of any party and an exciting, winsome personality to prove it--a real social butterfly.

Yet Gloria knew the truth. It was reality as she perceived it. She felt alone, frustrated and pessimistic about the future. Her self-image had hit rock-bottom. She knew life had much more to offer but in her own mental space she had no room to manoeuvre. She felt stuck and hemmed in, with no real opportunity to grow.

But somehow the smile had never left her lips during the entire ride home this afternoon. Things were changing, on this very day.

As Gloria got off the train at her park'n ride stop, she knew that everything would be different very soon. At least, it would appear so. In a couple of days she would be on the beach, soaking in the sun and, sipping a tropical rum punch, with all her problems left far, far behind.

'Who said escapism was not a window for change, a door of opportunity or a pathway to a bright future? No harm in trying ...' she reasoned to herself.

Two days later Gloria was indeed comfortably snug in an economy seat sailing high above the clouds in a Boeing 737 en route to the beautiful Caribbean. None of her relatives or acquaintances could free themselves up on short notice, so she was making the trip solo. That was disappointing, but hardly a crisis. It's the price of spontaneous travel.

Gloria sunk into her seat as the aircraft cruised along gracefully at thirty-seven thousand feet. The sunshine streamed brightly through the window and the flight attendants cheerfully bantered about with passengers. She felt the tension beginning to seep out of her tired and tense body. She closed her eyes.

Tantalizing images began to dance before her mind's eye ... swaying palm trees ... lush green vegetation ... steel guitars and drums vibrating with calypso music ...windsurfing across the aqua waves ... breathing in the salty air ... the smell of fresh flowers carried along with a gentle evening breeze.

'Can't this plane go any faster?'

As she mentally lost herself in the hypnotic beauty of the Caribbean, Gloria slipped off to sleep with a soft smile of benediction across her face.

Gloria drifted in and out of a sweet sleep amid the droning of the aircraft's engines. Eventually the pilot's announcement brought her back to reality, as he called out his instructions in preparation for the descent and landing.

When she sat up, she glanced out the window to see the sun still high in the sky, shining down on the soft, fluffy clouds that looked like heaven's waiting room. The sleep had relaxed her even more. She couldn't stop smiling. Even the inevitable turbulence that started when the aircraft broke through the high cloud cover felt like a playful shake from God's hand.

Gloria rehearsed her plan for arrival with eager anticipation. She would claim her luggage, hail a taxi, and check into her hotel in the heart of the resort area. As soon as she could change into her bathing suit, she would head into the water for a quick swim. Finally, she would find an outdoor beach café, with music, for a quiet relaxing dinner. That would be the perfect scenario to begin her vacation.

The pilot was a true professional and soon, he and his computers brought the aircraft down with a smooth uneventful landing. There was a spontaneous applause in the cabin. As the aircraft taxied to the gate, Gloria wondered what might be in store for her in the next ten days of sun, fun and relaxation that she was about to enjoy.

Her experiences at customs and immigration were all routine. She found her two checked bags easily and started moving towards the terminal door on the lower level to find ground transportation. As she approached the door, a man with an airport badge stopped her:

"Could I see your baggage claim ticket, ma'am?"

"Uh ... sure ... if I can find it. Is there a problem?"

"No problem ma'am ... just routine security ... I make sure everyone leaves with their own bag."

She handed him her claim ticket and without wondering too much why security was so imposing on this relaxed island paradise, she walked out the door.

Gloria looked around the outdoor concourse for the

transportation steward responsible for taxis. She could find no such comfort, but a swarm of taxicab drivers soon found her and began to offer all kinds of interesting incentives to jump into their particular cabs. She identified one whom she judged instinctively to be reasonable enough. She gave him her luggage and jumped into the back seat of the old Ford.

"To Calipo, please. I'm staying at the Biltmon ... do you know where it is?"

The driver put his foot to the gas pedal and sped off, but he neglected to turn on the meter ... by habit or design, she could not tell. He made no obvious gesture to respond to her rather trivial question. It might have been trivial for him but in her own ignorance, it was most important to her.

Gloria waited a few seconds, and then asked again:

"Do you know where the Biltmon is?"

"Anghuuuu ... " The driver sneezed.

That was all she got for a reply.

Gloria looked out the taxi window. Was there any way to tell which direction they were going ... towards the water or away from the water? She contemplated this question for a few minutes and since the only answer was non-descript, she tried one more time, now with a tinge of irritation in her voice.

"Really ... I do need to know. Do *you* know where the Biltmon is, or not?"

He finally glanced at her through the rearview mirror

and shook his head in disgust.

"What do *YOU* think, ma'am? Do you think you could spend nineteen years driving this rolling junkyard 'round this town and not know where de Biltmon is? Do you think that's possible? I know where de Biltmon is and if I was you ... I'd stay there."

Well, at least he had a tongue. She rolled the window down to get a swallow of fresh air after she yawned a couple of times.

"How much longer?" she asked.

"Be patient, ma'am ... what's you' hurry?"

"No hurry ... " she answered.

She finally concluded that he was probably driving her to the Biltmon, but since he wasn't exactly in a conversational mood, why not just sit back and enjoy the ride? Yet one of his earlier comments kept gnawing at her.

"What did you mean when you said ... I'd better stay there?"

A malicious smile formed on his lips as he looked at her through the rearview mirror.

"Stay or go ... makes no difference to me, ma'am ... but you'll soon find out for you'self what I mean."

With that he turned his radio up a full half turn, an indication that the conversation was finished.

Fine with her.

Gloria turned her attention back to the window. She

could see occasional palm trees on the side of the road. Yet the scene was far from idyllic. True ... this might be one of the more underprivileged neighborhoods in town, an example of the ubiquitous contrast in living conditions in the developing world. But the sight was still depressing.

One particular item in the visual landscape caught her attention. Almost every single window in each building--house, store, office or apartment--was covered with an iron grating or metal bars of some kind. From appearances, people were imprisoned in their own homes.

The rest of the scene was equally bleak. There was garbage everywhere, deserted paraphernalia from polystyrene cups and popcans to stripped automobile skeletons. Imagine the sounds, the smells, the squatters, the hundreds of preschool children just hanging around aimlessly, but probably not anxiously.

At least there is no snow here, Gloria thought, and the sun was still there to welcome her.

Eventually the cab pulled into the circular driveway of the Biltmon and the driver stopped at the door.

"Twenty-six dollars, ma'am."

Without trying to determine the equation the driver used to arrive at this, Gloria simply paid up quickly, adding a tip, and jumped out. The doorman reached for her bags and she checked in without difficulty or delay.

Her room was clean but quite ordinary, despite the

extravagance of the price. She reminded herself that she was in the tropics and she really had not come here for the room.

After all, since she first imagined this getaway, she had flirted with a vicarious swim in the tropical beach paradise of her own mind. It was now time for consummation.

The sun was just about to say 'goodnite' and Gloria was determined to get in that swim before dark. She slipped into her colorful bikini and covered it with a very loose cotton shirt. With sun glasses in place and towel in hand, she called the Concierge to find out where the beach was. Gloria was ready and eager. She was now feeling good. She felt free. Important. Indulgent. Sexy. This was living.

"I'm sorry ma'am but we've already closed the beachfront at the hotel ... I'm afraid you've missed it for today," the Concierge told her in a soft voice.

This was not the time to find out why the Hotel beach was closed, although still in adequate daylight.

"What about the public beach? Where is it? Is it close by?"

"Very close ma'am, but I would advise against visiting the public beach ... the time for ocean swimming really has passed us by for today, ma'am."

"You don't understand," Gloria answered. She tried to explain about gray black snow, winter chills, and her last minute vacation plans made with intent to restore sanity.

The Concierge obliged by patiently listening to her vent her frustration.

"I do understand, ma'am ... completely ... but I'm sure that a nice invigorating morning swim tomorrow will set the matter right. I'm afraid I must be firm against the idea of an early evening ocean swim. We really have had a run of bad luck at the public beach after five. I'm sure you understand, ma'am."

"I wish I did understand ... but thanks for the advice."

"I should add, ma'am ... the Hotel pool, of course, is open and you are more than welcome to use it."

"A chlorine pool I could have had back at the YMCA," she mumbled as she hung up the telephone.

The thought did run through her mind to go to the public beach anyway, but the ride from the airport had also taken some of the wind out of her emotional sail, so she decided against that idea, too.

Reluctantly, Gloria picked up the local paper and shuffled down to the poolside deck. She stretched out on a lounge chair and nonchalantly flipped through the few pages.

Her eye stopped at a summary side bar story on the news page. The headline read: "Homicide Rate Decreases". It went on to say that the murder rate had declined from twenty-five to twenty-three people.

What?

Although twenty-three murders in one year seemed

like a lot on an island this size, at least it was going in the right direction, she reassured herself. But then she realized that she had misread the story--the twenty-three people had been murdered last *quarter*, not last year.

Gloria gasped.

No wonder they close the beach so early. All of a sudden, it seemed like she could feel the gastric acid pouring into her stomach.

She was revived by the local Sports pages. Soccer was big here and a local hero was being celebrated for a hatrick in a big game of the inter-island competition. She revelled in nostalgia and regressed to the joys of childhood when she played beachball. That seemed so long ago.

Gloria went to dinner with a tiny knot in her stomach. Still, she was determined to enjoy her ten days in the sun. The maitre-d' seated her beside a lovely couple whom she discovered was from Oregon. As they chatted Gloria found out that they had been on the island for six days of a planned fourteen day vacation. Yet they were flying home the next day, seven days early.

"But why?" she asked.

"Well ... we've had enough. The weather has been great every single day ... but how many days can you spend in the lobby of a Hotel?"

Gloria jumped in.

"But this place is full of fabulous things to see. They

have hundreds of miles of sandy beaches. The rain forest is one of the lushest in the hemisphere. The cafés and museums are supposed to be superb. Did my travel agent lie to me?"

The tall bespeckled gentleman looked up and over his coffee mug to make deliberate eye-contact. His speech was slow and calculated.

"Probably not. I'm sure all of that's true ... but the big question is, who would be fool enough to actually venture out and see them? Certainly not us ... we're going home!"

He spoke as if he were delivering a graduate thesis defense.

Gloria was truly puzzled.

As she questioned them more and more, they told her their story. For six straight days they had spent every day moving from one hotel lobby to the next, lounging at the pool and eating at the hotel restaurant. It became clear that they were deathly afraid of going anywhere that didn't have strong tourist security in place.

Gloria concluded they must have suffered a bad experience that scared the daylights out of them. She asked them what in particular might have happened to them.

"Actually we've been lucky", the wife became less agitated and more animated. "Our strategy has paid off ... knock on wood. We've managed to stay out of any real trouble. But we've been lucky. So we're not keen to push it."

"Hmmmm ..." Gloria murmured.

After a time they excused themselves.

"We've got to finish packing". The wife seemed eager to take control. The husband was focused on Gloria.

"But I'm sure you'll have a marvellous time here. The weather is just gorgeous. Good luck, honey." He winked.

With that cynical reminder and wish, they made their way out of the restaurant.

Gloria sat drinking tea, trying to make sense of the last four hours. Surely this couple has overreacted. But twenty-three murders are just that -- twenty-three murders. In just three months, Gloria reminded herself.

She began to reconsider her own plans.

Originally, she had hoped to rent a car and perhaps team up with a couple of other adventurous people and drive around the island to see the sights. Now, she wasn't quite so sure of the prudence of that plan.

She wandered out to the hotel patio that overlooked the ocean and sank into a chair by the railing. The pounding ocean surf and the salt air were invigorating, and Gloria sat contentedly listening to the beat of steel drums coming from the hotel lounge. At ten-thirty she returned to her room and retired for the night.

Just as so many people had promised, the sun was shining and the sky was clear the next morning when Gloria went down to the open-air restaurant for breakfast. To rent the car or not? It's usually better to be safe than sorry. What to do? ... What to do?

She was ashamed to admit that fear conquered reason and she spent the first day of her ten day getaway planted in the hotel. She completed a routine circuit from her room to the pool, to the beach, to the lounge, and back to her room.

In the evening, Gloria noted that one of the hotels in the strip did have a casino and that tempted her at least momentarily. But surely her credit card didn't have the stamina to absorb a bad run at the blackjack table. Uncle Visa had a limit. After wandering around the casino for fifteen minutes, she found herself back on the deck of the hotel, listening to the crash of the surf and the muffled sounds of the local calypso band that was still entertaining in the lounge.

The next day she slept in until eleven. No point in getting up early to see the hotel lobby one more time. The pattern was easily established over the next few days. A prisoner in paradise. Was this really an escape? Eventually, she became disillusioned with the whole vacation experience and decided to return home earlier than planned.

Gloria checked out in disgust. Disappointed.

Her taxi driver was on time, for a change. He threw her bags into the trunk and no sooner were they winding through the narrow streets again, that he started whistling:

"*Don't worry, be happy ...*"

Gloria was quiet and pensive.

"Can you whistle, ma'am?" the cabbie asked, glancing into his rearview mirror.

"*No, I can't.*"

"Can you sing, ma'am?"

"*No, I can't.*"

"Can you smile, ma'am?"

"*No, I can't.*"

"Tell me ma'am ... Why worry? ... Be happy."

"*No, I can't.*"

"Is there *anything* you can do, ma'am?"

"I am beginning to wonder."

"That's your choice, ma'am."

He was finished. She felt it and knew it.

As Gloria sat reflecting on the plane coming home, she seemed to gain remarkable insight into her own life... It was pathetic, a life of pathos. But that was her *choice*.

She was coming home, still depressed. Nothing had really changed. The same office was there to greet her, the same lonely apartment, the same frustrations. But even more than all of that, she still had the same negative attitudes.

"*No, I can't.*" That was still her chant.

She needed a good mirror.

* * *

YOU CAN

You can! You can! Anyone can!
If only they affirm:
"I am! I am! I know that I can!
What I don't know, I'll learn."

From deep within it comes,
That affirmation clear.
No need for outside hope or help
To earn a presence here.

This is your time and place -
Whate'er your circumstance.
The key is yours, 'tis in your hand,
To use by choice, not chance.

So whoever you are, be you.
Wherever you are, be there.
Whatever you wish ... achieve, become!
Unlock all that and more.

—A.C.S.

The Compliance Test

Recall that this book is a prescription.
Having read this tale, you may experience some "side effects."
*Take some time now to **describe** any of the possible "side effects" that you observe:*
–Dr. YES!

Inspiration ...

Entertainment ...

Challenge ...

Imagination ...

Breakthrough ...

Self-discovery ...

Crisis ...

Motivation ...

Humour ...

Increased appetite for ... YES!

YOUR PRESCRIPTION

TEN (10) LIFELINES OF HOPE

If you were falling into the abyss of negativism and defeat, with such poor self-image that all you could muster was **"NO! I can't"**, *then here are some lifelines to hang on to. Grab as many as you wish and hold on for dear life.*

1.   **You can forget.**
2.   **You can begin again.**
3.   **You can choose.**
4.   **You can change.**
5.   **You can try.**
6.   **You can fail.**
7.   **You can learn.**
8.   **You can become.**
9.   **You can forgive.**
10. **You can smile.**

Now you know, **"YES, I can!"** *You've arrested the fall. You have found a foothold from which to spring into action as you continue* **The Evolution of YES!**

−Dr. YES!

2

Strangers In The Night
("Anybody else but me")

> *The measure of whether you will be happy at any interval, or even when the game of life is near the end, depends on whether you have played at the game of your own choice or someone else's.*
>
> —A.C.S.

After all, office parties are designed to relax, and have fun, to mix and mingle, to build rapport and communicate. But not every employee does that easily. Bill Gingerelli certainly did not. He was a thirty-four year old accountant, as razor sharp as they come.

Bill worked hard all day long for Glick, Johnson & Weller, and he didn't begrudge doing it. But what he did resent was his mandatory attendance at company functions similar to the one tonight. It was the retirement party for one of the long time office managers. This was a semi-formal affair and it seemed like everybody was there.

Bill had nothing against his old office colleague, Ms. Trask. On occasion, they had even exchanged stories of weekend pleasantries that had brightened up many a Monday morning in the office corridors. No doubt her retirement would be a loss of no small magnitude both for Bill himself and the fortunes of G.J.&W. But what Bill could not fathom was the compulsory nature of these affairs.

On this night of all nights, he wanted to be somewhere else.

With his resentment boiling away, Bill started searching the hotel for a television. At least, that would be a poor substitute and 'half-a-loaf is better than no-loaf-at-all', he reckoned.

'Why did this little exercise in corporate decorum have to take place on precisely the same night that North Carolina was tipping off against UCLA to determine the NCAA Division I Basketball Championship?'

Bill checked his watch. The game would be starting in less than an hour and he wanted to strategically locate at least a couple of different television sets that he could repair to once the game began.

As he strolled the lobby and meeting rooms in search of the indispensable magic box, he was seized with a feeling of sublime injustice. How ironic. After watching twenty-four of the twenty-five televised NCAA tournament games, Bill was going to miss the Big One.

But the harder the televisions were to locate, the more Bill asked himself how much he really enjoyed working at G.J.&W. Maybe he ought to just leave the party anyway and let the chips fall where they may. They couldn't fire him, could they? Just for skipping out on a retirement party?

Bill wasn't ready to test this theory in any kind of meaningful way ... at least, not yet ... so he continued on his search with renewed vigor.

Finally, a nibble.

Behind the semi-closed door of the maintenance room he could hear the familiar buzz of the pre-game festivities. Bill took note of the number on the door and headed back to the party room.

For Bill Gingerelli, missing a basketball game was no small matter. He was obsessed with television sports, often watching two TV's simultaneously, set up side-by-side. He knew all four major league sports and the respective players in astonishing detail. He had not missed an NCAA Championship game in many years, and he sure was not about to break his impressive record tonight.

But since he was here, why not get dinner out of the way? The sooner, the better. He dashed back to the food.

Once Bill made it back to the party he wandered over to the buffet table and grabbed a plate. He was in no mood to converse or socialize. He would endure what he could not enjoy. That's survival. At least he did enjoy eating. And you had to hand it to them, the food was always great at these sentimental little gatherings.

So with a plate burdened with some Greek salad, cold

cuts and a giant pickle in one hand and a cold cider in the other, Bill found an empty table and sat down.

Bill knew most of the people who were there by name, and most of the rest he recognized. But he simply was not in a gregarious mood. They were his colleagues in the office, but only *inside* the office doors. Otherwise, he could not care less about this crowd.

He practiced accounting by day, but his real life was sports. He was more interested in Shaq, the Braves, Mario Lemieux, and the Buffalo Bills. They were more than just his heroes. His biography was being chronicled on the sports pages. There he experienced agony and ecstasy. He loved it.

As he was finishing the salad, a tall lady he didn't know sat down at his table:

"I hope I'm not disturbing you ... I just hate eating while standing."

"No ... go ahead ... there's lots of room."

"Thanks. Do you work with Gail Trask?"

"I suppose I do, although not directly. How about you?"

"Well, I'm not from this office. I've spent the last six years in the San Francisco office. But I was in town, and they said this would be a good place for me to meet people. My name is Laura. And yours?"

Her personality was so spontaneous and effusive. She seemed so naturally warm and radiant and carried herself with much poise. Bill was sensitive to her camaraderie and for a moment felt like he belonged there, the right person, in the right place, at the right time. He thought about standing up to respond, but he didn't.

"Hello, Laura ... I'm Bill Gingerelli. I work in Contracts. But don't let me hold you back from your dinner. The roast beef looks great."

Laura glanced over at Bill's plate then quietly stole a moment of eye contact that ushered in gentle smiles that seemed to originate from a common trigger.

> *"Strangers in the night, exchanging glances,*
> *Wondering in the night, what are the chances*
> *We'll be sharing love*
> *Before the night is through ... "*

It was a classic moment deserving a classic song by a classic voice. But no one sang. There was only the sound of silence in the air.

Bill was sitting at right angles to Laura. In as casual a way as he could manage, he shifted his chair about a foot so he could get a better angle. Laura blushed and retreated to finishing off her coleslaw while Bill watched her intently from the corner of his eye.

'What an intriguing addition to the office', he thought. Suddenly he perceived an adequate reason for being at the party.

Bill was not presently engaged in any serious romantic

liaisons, although he had dated many women over the years. None of the relationships had gone anywhere and more than one of Bill's casual dating acquaintances had put their finger on exactly what they perceived to be the problem.

"You're just not here, Bill," was a common refrain. "Even when you're here, you're still not here."

To his credit, Bill was not so cold and hard in his emotional repertoire that he did not recognize at least the partial truth of these allegations. But he was in denial of his obsession, oblivious to the real cost to his personal life. After an eight month dating relationship, one of his girlfriends had put him off bluntly.

"Bill, if you ever sell your television sets ... give me a call." She was gone.

That one hurt, but Bill didn't think there was anything at all wrong with keeping busy by watching things you enjoy. After all, sports was for real men. Winning was everything. At least there was something to make him feel real good and to cheer about, all year round. It did not interfere with his job and he would definitely cut back, he protested, if any relationship did get serious.

'Besides, there were no decent women left out there anyway. Why bother going through the drill and never having a parade? Why risk a disappointing or even disastrous evening out, when Penn State vs Notre Dame was on television? That's a guaranteed climax and without any personal power play.'

But Bill's romantic sensibilities were not so far gone tonight that he did not enjoy a long second and third look at Laura. She had a wide-eyed, scrubbed innocence.

Before long, Bill took up conversation with her that was effortless and wildly funny. They both had exactly the same sense of humor. He soon concluded that maybe this retirement party was not going to be a complete dud after all.

He and Laura sat by themselves sharing the most unforgettable retirement party stories they could recall. Their body language was direct, mutual and clear. They inched closer and closer together each time they became more animated.

Eventually the speeches began, an unwelcome interruption to the real communication taking place in the room that night. The crowd was silenced and everyone heard about the wonderful contribution that Ms. Trask had made to the success of G.J.&W.

As the speeches droned on, Bill and Laura could not resist exchanging a conspiratorial wink and grin.

Laura looked at her watch. Bill wasn't the only one who had an engagement to keep. In much the same fashion as Bill's sportsmania, Laura had an equal, if not greater devotion to the movies. She was a big fan and tonight was the big night.

Tonight was the night for the annual Academy Awards and Laura had no intention of missing the good parts.

She wanted to be back in her hotel room by ten to watch host David Letterman be his funny self and practice his own brand of narcissism, laughing incessantly at his own jokes. Hopefully she would see her favorite actress, Whoopie Goldberg, make her comic faces as she exposed her big white teeth to punctuate her big, broad grin that has become a trademark. Would Apollo 13 dominate this year? Laura was enamored by Tom Hanks and had even seen the movie five times already.

Fortunately, tonight she would not have to wait. The formal retirement ceremonies were brief and to the point.

Laura was thrilled.

After the gifts had been given to Gail Trask and the speeches made, the patrons hung around to dance and finish their remaining drinks and nibble more hors d'oeuvres.

Bill and Laura chose to linger on even a little longer at the makeshift bar. Bill handed Laura a Sprite as he ordered a lite beer. They drifted over to the edge of the dance floor. Their conversation had been warm, pleasant and engaging.

Then Bill glanced at his watch and all of a sudden things got a little bit awkward. Both of them became acutely time conscious. Bill figured the first half of the basketball game would be almost over, while Laura figured that they had probably already dispensed with all the minor Awards and were about to embark on the biggies.

They had a simultaneous conflict of mutual interest.

This pre-occupation was doing nothing at all for the quality of the conversation, but still they lingered.

Bill had to admit that it had been years since he had spent as pleasurable an evening as he had, chatting with Laura. She was an exceptionally engaging young woman, definitely someone that he wanted to track down at the very next opportunity. But would it be too late?

Certainly Laura seemed to be enjoying herself. She had revealed so much about herself and so quickly.

Bill liked everything he heard.

Laura looked at her watch again.

"Do you have to go?" Bill choked on his words as he was torn by his own attraction and distraction.

Laura tried to pass the buck and avoid her own equivocations. She did not want to buck the pass that she was sensing all night and ruin her own expectations.

"I thought *you* had to go?"

"I do," Bill answered, "I really want to see the second half of the basketball game."

"I would not mind getting back for the Academy Awards myself."

They both looked away in shame. They knew their hearts were resonating, their spirits bonding, their hormones pumping. But they each needed a media fix that overwhelmed them even at this moment. They were enveloped in a cloud of vicarious social habit. Their heroes.

The thrill was all back there on television. How could they resist?

What was the next appropriate move? So much to do and so little time. But the time was not yet. It would be too much, too soon and yet too little, too late. They both vacillated.

Bill sliced the air as he choked on his words.

"Okay ... It's been such a pleasure meeting you. I enjoyed every minute of it. I guess I'll see you around the office. How often do you come in from San Francisco?"

Laura looked at Bill with unspoken expectation. She started to make her way to the coat rack. Bill quickly followed.

"Well ... this is the second time in six years. But I'm sure ... I'll be back some time."

Her voice rose on the last word as if she were asking a question and not giving an answer. Bill let this bit of news sink in for a moment. She really did have a radiant smile. He could look her up when he was in San Francisco. But when would that be? He had been to San Francisco only once in his life.

All the pre-game hype guaranteed that North Carolina vs UCLA was going to be a classic. He hadn't even bothered to set up his VCR to tape the game. It had to be live. He had to see at least the latter half.

Bill helped Laura with her coat and then he put on his own.

Laura suddenly remembered something

"Oh ... I forgot my Daytimer. It must be back at the table."

"I'll get it."

When Bill found the soft leather binder he was sorely tempted to look in and find her address and phone number, but he was still in plain view where she could see him. So he handed her the binder.

Neither really wanted to leave. They stood awkwardly for a while, and finally, Laura spoke with hesitation:

"I don't suppose you'd care to join me for a nightcap. Maybe we can find a place that is showing both the game and the Academy Awards."

Bill smiled. He wondered what his problem was. Of course he wanted to join her for a drink. It was the best offer he had received in months, if not years. But for some queer reason UCLA and North Carolina had been permanently etched in his brain, and the thought of trying to track down the game at a lounge was a non-starter. He could miss the whole thing. He searched his brain for an alternative but none was forthcoming.

"Uh ... I'd love to Laura ... I really would ... but tonight is just not the best night."

Bill could not believe what he had just said.

"How about coming over to my place?" He seemed to bite those words.

He had to say something but he knew the chances that Laura would accept were non-existent. Too risky, perhaps too soon. They were so near and yet so far. Their own obsessive agendas propelled them on courses that would not converge ... at least not here and not now. They were both out of control, out of touch with themselves and their own innate passions. They were each living in somebody else's world.

"Maybe next time."

Laura managed a weak smile and drifted out toward the door, waving goodbye to someone else she knew.

Bill drove home deeply disturbed. He thought about turning around and going back, but he didn't. He felt sad and glad, bad and mad, all at the same time.

Before long he was sitting in front of his television set, and when he turned the game on it was all tied up 45-45 with seven minutes left in the third quarter. Bill opened a bag of chips, got a diet coke out of the fridge, and sat transfixed as the game progressed.

For the next hour he was immersed in his true love and forgot all about Laura. He was transposed in time and space as he got caught up in every turnover, every penetration, every rebound. The game went into overtime.

A close finish in a championship game is hypnotic and compelling. He enjoyed it all but after the game he returned to his real personal space with his lost encounter.

'What if ... ?' That was the inevitable speculation.

As he settled into bed that night he could hardly sleep. He lay there in the moonlit darkness, his mind adrift with thoughts of Laura. Did he really spend this critical evening watching basketball while his heart-throb drifted away into the night?

He had no idea that by now he had been forgotten. Laura was herself asleep, dreaming of her *Tom Hanks.*

Sweet dreams.

Bill awoke with a song echoing in his head:

"Born to lose ... I've lived my life in vain
All my dreams have only brought me pain ... "

He had lost, again. So did Laura. They were both in tune with third parties ... but not with themselves. They were just fans.

* * *

THE FANS

The fans, they cheer the victors on,
They shout, they scream with glee.
But players, they enjoy the thrills -
Both agony and ecstasy.

The fans who live vicariously,
Inevitably lose.
They experience no personal pride,
But that's the life they choose.

The fans, they take no trophies home,
To truly call their own.
Their barren lives can pass them by
In vain oblivion.

Those fans, jumping in the balcony,
May need a wake up call:
'Tis time to get involved with 'ME'
'My thing', 'my game', 'my ball'.

Life is for living, you're counted in -
'Tis no spectator sport.
You can come down, you can join in.
So own your place on center court.

—A.C.S.

The Compliance Test

Recall that this book is a prescription.
Having read this tale, you may experience some "side effects."
*Take some time now to **describe** any of the possible "side effects" that you observe:*
–Dr. YES!

Inspiration ...

Entertainment ...

Challenge ...

Imagination ...

Breakthrough ...

Self-discovery ...

Crisis ...

Motivation ...

Humour ...

Increased appetite for ... YES!

YOUR PRESCRIPTION

TEN (10) STEPS TO STARDOM

If you said **"Anybody else but me"**, *then take these steps to lead you from the spectator gallery right on to center stage where you can be the star.*

1.	**Choose your game.**
2.	**Learn the rules.**
3.	**Get your gear.**
4.	**Go to the park.**
5.	**Find a coach.**
6.	**Rehearse your moves.**
7.	**Study the masters.**
8.	**Focus your attention.**
9.	**Join a team.**
10.	**Play to win.**

So you made the team. You're a key player. Now you can insist on **"Anybody, including me"**. *Strive ardently to win and so obtain the prize.*

–Dr. YES!

3

Walking Boots

("I should")

*There is no substitute anywhere for the conscience,
the conviction, the passion that allows you to know
what you should do, what you need to do,
and then constrains you to do it.*

—A.C.S.

'To be or not to be?' How often had Debbie asked herself that same question in the past few years. She could never find an answer. To be *what* ... she was never sure. But she was forever questioning or doubting being a *lawyer*.

Debbie glanced up at the clock on the wall. She was angry. The same old depressing story was repeating itself one more time. But what could she do? She felt used. She seemed trapped.

On his way out the revolving door, at minutes to five on this beautiful Friday afternoon in May, Edward Greendale, Q.C., a senior partner of Pierce & Jones, had just done it again. Without saying a word, he had recklessly tossed eleven legal depositions on Debbie's desk with a vulgar passing grunt and presumably, the unspoken understanding that they be reviewed and briefed, ready to present first thing Monday morning.

"See you on Monday," one of his partners shouted down the hall.

Greendale then breezed out of the office, opened the door of his shiny metallic gray Audi and slipped callously into the driver's seat. He revved the engine, turned down the window and with the radio booming the latest Michael Bolton hit, eased the car into the weekend rush hour traffic.

"T.G.I.F.", he muttered to himself. "Thank God, it's Friday."

Debbie stared at the depositions and then again at the clock. Was this for real? Another occasion to either quit or lose her sanity.

She was silently cursing the pretentions of the demanding and insensitive brute she had for a boss. He cared for no one and for nothing but the game of tennis.

Edward was not even good at tennis but he was challenged by it and was determined to improve his standing at the country club. He had already given up on his erratic golf swing, only to find that he did not have the stamina for racquetball. He never learned to swim.

But he thought he had found his forté when he took up tennis last year. At least he had qualified for the posted standings at the club. He believed he was destined for the top before the end of the year. He was deceiving himself since he weighed too much, his corrected vision was poor and his reflexes too slow. And he was only forty three.

Amateur? Not even that. Immature? At times. But he believed he knew best.

As for Debbie, it would not be so bad simply having to endure a never ending apprenticeship at this firm. But with a narcissistic partner constantly sporting a superiority complex, it was becoming intolerable. If only somehow she could feel sure that there was a faint glimmer of hope for progress in her legal career.

But three long years after her initiation, Debbie was still tediously hunched over her desk checking the leases, clause by clause. She reviewed contracts and other documents for case references, completed boiler plate clauses, affixed seals, inserted dates and witnessed signatures. She also managed the due process and execution.

Edward Greendale and his partners were living the professionals' dream, including their good standing at the best country clubs across town.

Debbie knew that not every three-year lawyer at Jones & Pierce was still on permanent photocopy duty like her. Some of them had angled their way into court as a foot soldier for one of the Pierce & Jones' great legal generals. A few of her colleagues had gone on from there to single-handedly carry the ammunition in the occasional precedent or other major case that had to be won.

When a rookie finally made the grade, and when he or she had eventually acquired the status of a trusted comrade-in-arms by winning a big case for a big client, the soirée that followed was usually loud and long. Debbie would feel flattered just to be invited.

Debbie was no party-pooper. She had attended many of these social bulldozer events. She was convinced that 'paying her dues' included the painful humiliation of watching others, lawyer after lawyer, leave behind the life of the legal concubine, a life in which Debbie was still deeply immersed.

The eleven depositions sitting on her desk made that perfectly clear.

She glanced once more at the clock on the wall and whispered in disgust as she flipped the file cover of the deposition on the top of the pile. Just by the sheer size of each one, Debbie figured that she had at least eight hours of work in front of her to get them ready for Monday morning.

She would have to come back to the office tomorrow.

But she had made her own plans for this weekend. After all, she did have a life outside the office, her real life. She planned to be up early to drive to the Lake on this Saturday morning. She was going to help her mother plant tomatoes, carrots and squash in the back garden.

That new mountain of work before her now meant Friday night was going to be another long night at the office, with pizza and Diet Coke to keep her company.

Tonight she was not sure how exciting it truly was to be a lawyer ... unless you enjoyed eyestrain and migraines and had an insatiable appetite for paperwork. She was sure she did not qualify, and perhaps she did not even belong.

Debbie got up from her desk and walked over to the bottled water cooler. She usually repeated this ritual dozens of times a day to get some temporary relief from the crushing boredom that sometimes never subsided when she was working. But today she drank an extra sixteen ounces of nature's beverage in hope of cleansing her soul from imminent vocational despair.

She reflected on her professional barrenness and tried to account for the apparent drought, as she leaned against the wall of the nearly vacant office.

These career misgivings were not a recent development. Debbie had actually resisted the idea of becoming a lawyer right from the first time her father had broached the subject.

Becoming a lawyer had been his idea, not hers. But like waves pounding against a breaking wall, this ambitious immigrant had eventually worn his daughter down with the irresistible logic that fathers everywhere somehow manage to carefully tuck away for just such an occasion.

It became an absolute insistence from him that she must first acquire something to fall back on. She must make preparations for the future. After all, lawyers get a ticket to the good life, that great American dream that he only got a glimpse of when he migrated to these United States of America.

The dream beckons like the North Star in the mental canopy of all the immigrants who endure struggle and hardship, but finally, through the circumstances of chance or sacrifice, manage to pass the Statue of Liberty and enter 'the land of the free and the home of the brave.'

Debbie was not immune to the power of a logical argument. She relented in her Junior year of college, and wrote the LSAT to gain a right of passage. She then applied and was accepted into Columbia Law School.

She could never forget the expression of joy on her father's face when she told him the news of her acceptance. That almost made up for the three years of academic bewilderment that she went on to suffer at the hands of the esteemed professors at Columbia's Faculty of Law.

Even in her Senior year, it seemed like her classmates were all chomping at the bit to slide into the legal fray and fearlessly serve before the bar of justice. Everyone around her was talking about clerkships and the best firms to work for or about postgraduate work.

Yet Debbie could never successfully overcome the feeling that despite her good grades, she was still on the outside of the real legal world, with her face as it were, pressed against the glass, looking in. She never quite felt like she belonged to the world of contracts and depositions, or torts and liabilities, or juries and verdicts. It truly remained completely foreign to her.

That feeling had never changed.

No wonder then that her current Friday night assignment was all that much more of a tedious grind. She really did not really wish to see one more deposition.

This was no fun at all.

The truth was that Debbie only felt completely at home, relaxed and engaged, when she was messing around with her guitar or her keyboard, trying to compose a new melody or just entertaining herself on any one of the five other instruments she naturally played by ear.

Music was something she had known from the *inside* all her life. She was a natural talent. It was her soul expressed.

In fact, when it came time to go to university, Debbie really wanted to go to a small local college, primarily so she could continue playing and singing in the little three piece band that she had put together two years before.

That group was her intimate family, by choice and by association. Margaret was a girl she met during a high school trip to France, and Zoran grew up in her neighborhood. He didn't say much but he could really play the guitar with finesse and style. He had developed quite a small fan club at some of the local coffee houses and summer fares.

Without any doubt Debbie had loved the whole music scene. It was for her a passionate and fulfilling experience. Whenever she finished singing and playing for an audience, it would take her a couple hours to get off the emotional cloud nine. There was always that tingle of excitement that went up and down her spine as she stroked her violin or belted out the songs and swayed to the rhythm of the bass guitar.

She enjoyed a wide repertoire, from classical to contemporary. Almost anything with rhythm or pitch or cadence could trigger her adrenals.

Music was passion. Music was life. Music was for Debbie. Today it now seemed far away and long ago.

Here she was, lounging against the office wall, depressed with just the thought of a huge stack of depositions patiently waiting on her desk. Yet Debbie's eyes started to shine momentarily and her lips parted in a warm smile at the pleasant memories of those carefree highschool concerts and the sublime feeling of singing songs she loved, for people who adored and loved her. How had it all gone so wrong?

Debbie made her way back to her desk humming Whitney Houston:

"I believe that children are the future ..."

Her desk looked as disorganized as a children's playroom. There were message slips, books, case reports, files and papers, randomly stacked on all four corners, with sticky notes hanging from every exposed surface. The new depositions sat there in the center in bright orange folders waiting to be read.

As she hesitatingly opened the first one, a flashing red light from the telephone caught her eye.

That was probably Greendale calling on his cellular from courtside to press home the urgency of these depositions and to make sure that Debbie had not strayed too far from the palatial offices of Jones & Pierce.

Debbie thought about ignoring the message, but she figured that listening to it would at least put off those depositions for a few minutes. Maybe she could even convey her disappointment by telepathy.

So she keyed in her password and retrieved the message on voice mail ... Surprise!

No, it was not Greendale at all. Debbie could scarcely believe who was calling her. How had he found her number? She replayed the message four times.

"No, not Zoran ... Zoran Ikenovic?" she shouted out.

She focused on the message she had just heard. Yes, Zoran was in town. Two years had gone by since he had last dropped in to entertain her with horror stories of life on the road. Not only was he in town, but he had an engagement tonight at the Holiday Inn just off the Interstate highway.

He was calling in desperation. He had a problem.

His lead singer had come down with the stomach flu.

Would Debbie be interested in filling in for the evening? Would she care to sing all the old songs and even tell all the old lines and get socially caught up?

That was the message.

Zoran left her his number at the hotel and said he needed to know by seven. They could rehearse for an hour and be on stage at nine.

Just the prospect was exhilarating.

Debbie started to dial his number without even hanging up the telephone. No way was she going to get the depositions finished by seven and she couldn't disappoint her mother.

But still, the very sound of Zoran's voice had put a flutter in her heart that she hadn't felt in years. All the old songs. On stage, again. Wow!

Debbie hung up the telephone. She tapped lightly on the desk with her nervous fingers, but even that sound was music to her ears and gave rhythm to her pulse. What titillation. What to do next? What to do now?

The depositions ... Crazy Greendale ... Her career ... The music she loved ... Zoran ... Her passion ... Her dad ... Her old guitar ...?

The more she thought about singing again, the more excited she got. Finally she decided she'd call her best friend Jo to see what Jo thought she ought to do. But as she was dialing Jo's number, a thought struck her.

'That's how I got in this mess in the first place, letting other people make the decisions for me.'

Suddenly a light went on inside. Passion ignited. She felt like her heart leapt out of her bosom and her feet were off the floor. She was drifting, flying, soaring ... above the clouds. At her command.

But what about Greendale? The mere thought of facing Greendale on Monday morning without the finished depositions put an immediate lump in her throat.

No, she had to get those depositions finished. But hang on a minute. Who's *the* boss?

She regained her composure.

'Was Greendale himself making a decision for me? Was he in fact telling me what to do? Was I listening to him because, yes, exactly *because I was not listening to myself*, my inner self?'

She kept thinking. She continued tapping with her fingers and now with her feet, but inside she was catapulted into space. Her space.

Was the threat of office punishment or reprimand a good enough reason to forego an experience she knew she was going to love? And for what? Depositions that she hated?

'To be or not to be?' This time the question was obvious and the answer was very clear.

"I know what I should do!" she screamed out.

She had just got in touch with her real self and thereby taken control. She sighed deeply.

Debbie imagined that the idea of singing in front of an audience after all this time would bring on a case of the nerves, but the thought of it didn't trouble her at all now. In fact, the sooner the better.

As she sat there at her desk she was undergoing an emotional metamorphosis, a cleansing.

The idea of performing again grew and grew, in her heart, to the point that denying it would be a denial of her truest self. She had cut herself off too many times from the deep inner longings of a soul alive.

No more.

She picked up the telephone and dialed Zoran's number.

"It's a deal." She concluded the reacquaintance.

'What about Greendale?' The question kept coming back.

"Well," Debbie muttered, "let the dead bury their dead. I want to live!"

That night Edward Greendale had a rude awakening. He was blown away as he sat drinking in the Holiday Inn lounge with a visiting friend from Australia. The special guest soloist was introduced ...

"Talented, vivacious, charming ... Debbie Pilarski!"

She began with:

"These boots were made for walking
And that's just what they'll do-
One of these days, these boots
Are gonna' walk all over you ..."

Their eyes made contact. Could this be for real?
Debbie was in control. She was passionate. She was doing
what she knew she *should* be doing at that moment.. Yes,
Pierce & Jones would never be the same, again.

Her dad might even be proud.

She was thrilled. Liberated.

* * *

YOUR STRIDE

Running, running, running,
You soon intend to stop.
Sometime you hope to turn around
And get things right side up.

You need not try to run and hide.
Only express what's deep inside.
You'll gain your own reward, indeed
Sooner or later, it's guaranteed.

You can refuse for sure, I know,
To follow that other agenda.
No one can walk within your shoes,
'Tis by your stride, you'll win or lose.

So, if you listen, you sure will hear:
Begone all doubt, and dispel fear.
If you would heed, you sure will live:
Dream inside, that's your prerogative.

—A.C.S.

The Compliance Test

Recall that this book is a prescription.
Having read this tale, you may experience some "side effects."
*Take some time now to **describe** any of the possible "side effects" that you observe:*

–Dr. YES!

Inspiration ...

Entertainment ...

Challenge ...

Imagination ...

Breakthrough ...

Self-discovery ...

Crisis ...

Motivation ...

Humour ...

Increased appetite for ... YES!

YOUR PRESCRIPTION

TEN (10) VOICES OF CONSCIENCE

If you keep saying 'I should' but struggle to convert that conclusion into action, take time to listen to the voices of conscience within. They will constrain you to do the thing you ought to do, the very thing you want to do. You should because ...

1. "It's the right thing to do."
2. "Someone is depending on you."
3. "Your gut says do it."
4. "You are the only one who can do it."
5. "You made a promise."
6. "It is expected of you."
7. "The Law demands it."
8. "It makes sense."
9. "There is no alternative."
10. "It's good for you."

Now you really know you should. "Action without thought could be fatal but thought without action is clearly futile." So act, now you know you should.

–Dr. YES!

4

Three Coins
In The Fountain
("If ...")

Reason calculates risk but passion alone conquers it.

—A.C.S.

Mike was always happy to shut down his software group for three days and fly out to Las Vegas. He could let off a little steam at the Tech World Trade Show that was held every year on the second weekend of November. This year as usual, he brought along his entire programming team hoping they would network effectively and get some new ideas.

New ideas? Yes, Mike was feeling guilty because he had not been keeping up lately. Group discussions had lacked the usual spark and excitement for which they were known in the company. Nothing new or hot was cooking internally. In the information age, knowledge is power and innovation is the key to ignition.

Mike himself was a master at networking. He was a bright gregarious technocrat who knew 'how to win friends and influence people'. He arrived a few days early in Vegas, specifically to unwind before the shop-talk got into high gear. He thought it really was an advantage to be relaxed and refreshed when all the high sales pitching and the subtle diplomacy began. These shows could often become both high-powered and high-pressured. This one was promising to be no different.

With a broad smile on his face, Mike stood in the open doorway looking out at the final preparations for the massive trade display being assembled on the floor. He began to imagine the tumult and uproar that would soon be evident on this high tech electronics stage.

There were hundreds of exhibitors at this show, with a vast collection of hardware and software innovations. Microsoft and Netscape were leading the pack with colorful arrays of synchronized displays. The keyboard wizards and electronic technicians were huddled in small groups everywhere.

This was the year of the Internet explosion and everyone wanted to capitalize. Billions of dollars were being effectively waged in a calculated gamble. Software warlords were in bitter feud for the relationship between the personal computer and the Internet. Would the consumer opt for a more sophisticated PC with integrated software to utilize the

Internet reservoir? Or would the popularity of surfing the net win out, with high powered web browsers to access and exploit that Internet data base with more interactive flexibility and much, much more?

It was a case of *déjà vu* for anyone who remembered Alfred Sloane and Henry Ford gambling over the consumer's wishes for the automobile of the future.

The stage was being set.

Row after row of exhibits were lined up all the way to the far wall. Exhibitors were busy pulling equipment out of boxes and wrestling ironically with the simple aluminum tubes used to hang the corporate banners. If only the budding mechanical genius assigned to the job could figure out how to put them together.

Mike started to stroll down the first aisle, checking out the keyboards, monitors, disc drives, printers, software packages and the myriad of interactive games, virtual reality and a host of other info-age equipment. He was careful to stay out of conversational range of the sales people.

It wasn't that Mike did not enjoy hearing about all the latest high performance gadgets, but this year he had bigger fish to fry. He was particularly alert and very focused. That's what a clear goal will do.

The soft leather briefcase that Mike was carrying contained the Beta version of a software program he had been writing, off and on, for over two years.

Mike managed a relatively large group of programmers for Elkotech, one of the communication giants. But the little gem he carried in this briefcase was all his own. It had been conceived, programmed, and debugged on his own time and at his own expense. It was a masterpiece of innovation that could impact the turf war in some small but significant way. He had brought it to the point where it now gleamed with a technical virtuosity that was breathtaking.

Mike had carefully documented the whole process. Not that he didn't trust Elkotech, but too many times in the past Mike had watched other programmers walk away empty handed when "intellectual property rights" cases were tried in court.

It was always better to be safe. Technically, it was also safer to be better, better than the competition. And yes, also better than your own company technocrats.

After fifteen years in the business, which in the computer world amounts to about five lifetimes, Mike had watched programmer after programmer step into the spotlight with their own creation, and after successfully floating the initial public offering to an eager investment community, make out like mere bandits. After all, in the corporate matrix, research is company property. Or is it?

Mike was positive that the four disks in his briefcase were going to create the type of innovation that had significant commercial applications. He was already imagining the possibilities. He had been putting out some feelers to see where the interest might be. Nibbles came in from both sides. He had already spoken to a financier who expressed an interest in floating a start-up company to market the software product. And he had heard from someone interested in buying the software outright.

Mike began dreaming... daydreaming of success, big success. *What if...?*

Mike wasn't sure which way to go. His secret dream was to shake off the shackles of Corporate America and get into a position where he could whistle his own tune. The very idea gave him a spinal tingle, but unfortunately it wasn't long before the doubts started to pound his brain.

He felt it would be a monumental risk to quit Elkotech, to jump headlong into the swelling waters of high tech entrepreneurship, no matter how much it appealed to him.

From Mike's vantage point, the risks were huge. They started with his children's education, progressed to the mortgage on his house, and jumped to retirement savings, health benefits, and all the rest of the financial stabilizers that Mike had carefully put in place. All of them would be vulnerable *if* he took the plunge.

What if he moved out on his own, and failed? What would his family say? Would his wife support him? What would his colleagues think? What would he do then? He kept asking himself the same questions. His spine chilled.

In the face of these disheartening risks, Mike thought that the most prudent thing to do would be to sell the program. He could realize a nice financial reward and be thankful that the process had gone so well. This would be the easy, low-risk alternative.

There was nothing to lose but a potential opportunity. And that's what all opportunity is, potential. Nothing ventured means nothing lost. True or false?

Cynics are quick to point out that 'happy is the one who expects or attempts little, for he or she is never disappointed'. But the real entrepreneurs cannot evade the challenging question '*what if...* ?'

The truth is that Mike's mind had been wildly double-tracking on both of his options for a solid six weeks. He wanted to make up his mind. And if all went well, that is exactly what he would do this weekend. That was his plan.

So he made more contacts as the show got off to an explosive start. There were simultaneous lectures, seminars, workshops, lunches, happy hours, informal meetings ... lots to see and touch, more to learn and take away from the exhibition floor. There was too much to do and too little time. From the very first morning, Mike was busy. Anxious too.

He listened well.

Then he mused. Confused.

There was such a strange irony. Mike was so typical of the many bright and ambitious space-age software technicians who make a good living developing algorithms that threaten to replace the human brain. These software packages exploit the information decision trees which reduce complex series of crossroads in mathematical logic into electronic binary states. These then translate into the 'on' or 'off' condition of semiconductors assembled on printed circuit boards. That is the fundamental principle of the computer design which has found widespread application in all spheres of modern life and as such has changed the world.

Mike was an expert at creating and manipulating these decision trees, identifying the choices that lead to the end result that the computer program was designed to deliver. But that was all theoretical and mechanical, all electronic, and inanimate. It was nothing personal. No value judgments were involved.

The human element makes all the difference.

Today Mike faced a different type of crossroad, a personal decision tree. In that, he was alone.

The final evening of the Trade Show arrived. It was time for a private resolution. Would he take a calculated risk?

Later that evening ...

With a piano tinkling in the background, Mike and a couple of his closest non-Elkotech friends, Gary and Ed, were sitting at the bar working on a round of B-52's and a pitcher of beer, musing about the scenario that Mike had just described.

The pianist was playing a classic tune:

"Three coins in the fountain,
Each one seeking happiness.
Three coins in the fountain,
Which one will the fountain bless?"

"So what did you say?" Ed asked.

"What could I say?

With that much money on the table ... I had to accept the offer.   They have their lawyers drawing up the paperwork. We're meeting again in their suite at ten o'clock."

"Tonight?" Ed wanted to be sure.

"Why so fast?" Gary queried, "There is no reason to be moving this quickly."

"Well," Mike answered, as he stroked his beard, blinked rapidly and rubbed the back of his neck. "I want it over with. My mind has been racing like crazy. I've gone back and forth enough. Besides, they put a good offer on the table. I'd be a fool to turn down $65,000. I don't know its worth. A bird in the hand is worth two in the bush, isn't it?"

"Two in the bush? Come on, Mike." Gary leaned forward and looked Mike straight in the eye. "You sound like a twenty year old. Surely you, of all people, know that if they offered you $65,000, then the program must be worth maybe $650,000 or more. This isn't a hobby for these people. They aren't in the habit of overpaying when they acquire new stuff."

Gary looked over at Ed for some support. Ed looked away. He knew exactly how Mike felt. He had felt the same way himself six years ago when he went through exactly the same process.

But Gary was adamant.

"Come on, you guys. Mike, you've put in your time. There is never a perfect time to get in the driver's seat. Your ship just came in ... this is what you've been dreaming about for years. Well it's here. Now. Right now. You've got to jump on it. Spin-off your own company. The time usually comes in everyone's life when you have to take a calculated risk. Yes, risk! Please ... $65,000? ... that's probably about eighteen dollars an hour when you look at all the time you put into the project. Where's your backbone? Look. if I were you ..."

"But you're not me." Mike interrupted before Gary insulted him any further.

"Been there, done that." Ed mumbled the old cliché to himself. He did not know what to think.

Mike looked at Gary for a long thirty seconds, then seeing that it was nine forty-five already, he pulled out his wallet and threw two twenty dollar bills on the table.

"Thanks, guys ... it's on me." Then he walked out of the lounge and headed for the elevator bank.

He had made up his mind. There was no turning back.

That evening, Mike signed a contract to sell his pet program for $65,000. His hands trembled, his palms sweat and his heart raced. He still wondered "*what if* ...?"

But beyond that was the unknown.

Not for long.

Three months after this transaction was completed, the details of the new software applications were made public. Elkotech became very interested. They saw major commercial advantages. They did not challenge Mike's intellectual property rights but made a fast bid and bought out the small company for $5.3 million just to get access to Mike's innovative program.

Five point three million dollars.

As for Mike himself, upper management lost faith in him. He received a small citation but no promotion. He was the only loser.

"*What if* ... ?" Mike still wondered.

What if he invented something else?

He is still trying.

*   *   *

CALCULATED RISK

Life's not a gamble,
'Tis a calculated risk ...
Sooner or later,
For worse or better,
You're trapped.

You must dive,
You must dare
Beyond the known,
Outside the sure,
To take a chance ...
On you.

Where you cannot see,
You must believe.
What you do not know,
You must assume.
And ...
When you dare not fail,
You still must try.

There is never failure
In trying.
So ...
Take that Risk on Yourself --
And win BIG.

—A.C.S.

The Compliance Test

Recall that this book is a prescription.
Having read this tale, you may experience some "side effects."
*Take some time now to **describe** any of the possible "side effects" that you observe:*
                                                            –Dr. YES!

Inspiration ...

Entertainment ...

Challenge ...

Imagination ...

Breakthrough ...

Self-discovery ...

Crisis ...

Motivation ...

Humor ...

Increased appetite for ... YES!

YOUR PRESCRIPTION

TEN (10) RISK QUESTIONS

If you are faced with challenge and opportunity and keep equivocating with a conditional "If ...", then ask yourself the following questions and pursue the answers until the path forward becomes clear.

1. **"What's the worst that could happen?"**
2. **"What are my options?"**
3. **"If not now, when?"**
4. **"Can I afford not to?"**
5. **"What's the long-term view?"**
6. **"What do I control?"**
7. **"Who else is involved?"**
8. **"Is a midcourse correction possible?"**
9. **"Is there a precedent to learn from?"**
10. **"What if it all works out?"**

*Success is not in taking the right risks but in connecting with the right passions. Then an exciting **life of risk** is worth it, win or lose.*

–Dr. YES!

5

Rich Uncle Clyde

("I would like to")

*Much of what we achieve is the result of a process
that begins in the head with an idea, migrates down
into the heart as a feeling, a passion, and which then
radiates into the hands to produce action.*

—A.C.S.

Henry and his wife Jackie were edging along the Lower Madison Expressway at about five miles per hour. A tremendous traffic snarl was jamming up the afternoon rush hour. They were stuck behind a big oil tanker that was creaking, at times groaning, and lurching forward in a jerky stop-and-go pattern. Occasionally it would spew out great clouds of diesel exhaust right into the grill of the beige Renault Alliance that Henry was driving.

"For the last time, Henry, can't we wind the windows up?" Jackie was at the end of her tether. She was exasperated. She could hardly resist trying to hold her breath to save her life. At least, that's how it seemed.

"I told you enough times already. I hate saunas."

Jackie chose to recoil. She would say no more.

Henry turned up the volume of the stereo.

The Alliance was equipped with air conditioning, but the temperature coil was on the blink, and the air conditioning unit was blowing out stale air that was no cooler than the blast furnace they were sitting in. Henry had therefore resorted to keeping both windows wide open. By now, Jackie could actually taste the diesel fumes. But Henry insisted that they had little choice. It was either that unavoidable pollution or risking suffocation under the blazing summer sun. Jackie contended that the fumes were unbearable, and the noise pollution could not even be neutralized by the animated rhythm of Bob Marley's reggae on cassette.

They both elected to sit in mutual silence, maintaining an uneasy truce. They were afraid that if either one of them spoke, the interaction would quickly degenerate into a catfight of truly ugly proportions.

They were surely not alone. This was the afternoon rush hour. Who knows what was going on behind each steering wheel or the cabins framed by tinted glass? Sometimes, compared to other options, silence is golden.

Their final destination was a big contributor to the loud marital reticence that had befallen the front benchseat of the Alliance. It was the reason they had willingly foregone the dry cool air of their fourteenth floor apartment and piled into the rusty vinyl-seated family car in the first place. They did not easily or concertedly elect to boil in the afternoon sun on a sizzling asphalt highway. In truth, they were on their way to see Henry's uncle, Clyde.

So weather and traffic aside, as Henry sat drenched in sweat and hopelessly mired in highway gridlock, his uncle was uppermost on his mind. He could tolerate the physical pollution but he was facing more emotional pressure that was consistently straining his nerves and even his marriage.

His wife Jackie was impatient and frustrated. Henry had not been in her good books lately. She was tagging along only to keep the peace, but it had become a strained peace. If only she were in control, things would be so much different.

Henry was quite a patient man, but this Uncle Clyde-affair was becoming annoying and ridiculous.

None of the rest of the family, bless their atherosclerotic hearts or their diabetic kidneys, had made it past seventy-five. But Uncle Clyde, the younger brother of Henry's deceased maternal grandmother, was still galloping through the Indian summer of his sunset years. He had already survived two heart attacks and was now going on eighty-seven. Yet he felt alive and in control. Far from becoming frail and listless, his mind was still alert and perceptive and his speech articulate. In fact, Uncle Clyde was still bursting with ideas and grand plans.

Uncle Clyde had a grip on life, a tenacity for

enjoyment that was just about driving young Henry crazy.

It was not that Henry didn't have a warm regard for his great uncle. To suggest otherwise was sure to bring on a venomous attack from this jealous nephew, something his wife Jackie was all too familiar with.

But the sad fact was that Henry, in contrast, was a typical middle aged man with a bulging abdomen and gray, thinning hair. He was himself closing in on forty-five. He had casually surveyed all the great enterprises that ultimately lead to financial prosperity and had settled on one for himself that was a very low road indeed. The road was so low that it passed right over the headstone of his dear Uncle Clyde.

There lay the truth that Henry had never admitted to anyone, much less his wife of twenty-two years.

Jackie had done everything she could conceive of to encourage, support, cajole and at times even blackmail her irresponsible mate to get his act together. After they both finished college, they were married and blessed with three beautiful children. She anchored their household with love and proficiency.

Henry seemed to drift and stagger between office jobs that frustrated any career development. His single attempt to take a bold initiative was a short-lived experience with Direct Selling from their home. He took charge and would not let Jackie get too involved with the business.

He joined a great multinational marketing organization with a good reputation and strong support for their field force. The company provided impressive incentives with shocking cash bonuses, company-paid leased automobiles for consistent productivity and exotic convention travel, free for large numbers of proven achievers. They provided colorful recognition and an opportunity to make a real difference in the lives of others.

It was the chance of a lifetime for a struggling, middle-class, family-man like Henry, but he blew it.

He was too stubborn to give Jackie room to participate and grow. He was too proud to do the simple things consistently and he was too weak to circumvent the initial difficulties on his learning curve. He drifted away and sank right back into mediocrity. He lost faith and confidence in himself.

Now he entertained a secret plan. At least, he thought it was a secret.

Whenever Henry started to wax sentimentally about how close he was to his Great Uncle, Jackie would roll her eyes in great sweeping arcs of exasperation. Granted, Uncle Clyde was an extremely wealthy man. It was also true that Henry was his sole remaining close relative. But Jackie was sickened by the infantile attitude of wishful thinking that had seized her husband. She was definitely losing all her residual respect for Henry. In her mind, it was the worst kind of ambulance-chasing morbidity, to sit around waiting for Uncle Clyde to go to his final reward.

This interlude of passive suspense had been going on for over a decade.

All these years they had been ingratiating themselves to Uncle Clyde at every opportunity. Henry saw to that. Birthdays, Thanksgiving, Christmas, Easter, Labor Day and every other holiday on the calendar--they were all religiously observed with Uncle Clyde.

There were cards, gifts, boxes of his favorite Cuban cigars. The two adolescent girls gave exclusive piano recitals for the honored guest, while Jackie was reminded to bake his favorite Mennonite pumpkin-pie recipe. Even seventeen year old Henry Jr. got in on the act. He would cut and style Uncle Clyde's hair and shave and pamper his face with Lagerfeld's best.

The kids enjoyed the treats. They thought their uncle was a sweet and kind-hearted old-man whom they could emulate. They told him so everytime they got a chance. But Uncle Clyde was not fooled by the attention. Every once in a while, Jackie could swear that he gave her a knowing wink.

The truth was that no one knew exactly how much money Uncle Clyde had stashed away, or who he planned to leave it to. Jackie figured that the Humane Society would get most of it. But suggesting any of this to Henry had a tendency to threaten turning the marriage into a World Wrestling Federation Main Event, so Jackie had stopped talking about it long ago.

Still, the situation was corroding some crucial support beams in the marriage, not to mention Henry's mental state. Yes, Jackie was tagging along for peace sake, but she was losing respect and had already began emotionally withdrawing from Henry.

Today the kids were away at summer camp, so the odd couple had decided to make a home visit. This was no needy house call, for they always emerged with far more goodies than they took with them. Kids or no kids, the visits were fun.

Today, the experience of just getting there was leaving much to be desired.

As the car eased around a sharp bend, Henry's eye caught a picturesque view of the horizon beyond an open field. It seemed like there had been some rain earlier, at least over yonder in the distance. What was left as a reminder was the beautiful arched rainbow silhouetted against the sky in the north. It was a welcome sight amidst the noise and smoke pollution.

Henry could not resist.

"Look Jackie, do you see that?"

Jackie jumped as if she were dozing off and looked out. The enchanting colors were delightful and she took a deep breath.

"Aah ... what a treat. I needed that."

"I need more than that. What's a rainbow without the

pot of gold?" Henry chuckled to himself.

"There you go again. When you're not wishing upon a star, you're dreaming of a pot of gold. Truly, 'if wishes were horses, beggars would ride'. You're something else."

Her sarcasm was chilling.

"What's wrong with dreaming? Remember Joseph? The dreamers inherit the future. Let me dream. I too, have a dream."

"Henry, please don't get me started. There are dreams and and then there are dreams. Some dreams are nothing more than wishful thinking. They are castles in the air, mere fantasy. Like delusions of grandeur. They remain in the brain."

"What's wrong with the brain?"

Jackie raised her voice.

"I believe that the brain has imagination but no passion. It needs blood to survive but it does not pump its own. Only the heart can generate the flow. That's when the dream travels eighteen inches to transform the world. Desire, commitment, focus ... these passions of the heart take hold of the product of real imagination and ignite it to consume the whole person. Then you get ablaze and the heat and light set the environs aglow and cause the future to happen."

"You're always talking about the heart. Why get so emotional?"

"The heart is everything. You can be brain-dead and still be alive, but it is impossible to be heart-dead and even exist. No wonder the Greeks called your inner self, your *heart*. This is real life. *No heart, no life*. That's so true. When all is said and done, life is first and most ... heart. Where is your heart, Henry?"

"I must have left it in San Francisco."

How glib. They were miles apart as usual.

By now, the rainbow was out of sight but they would not soon forget that brief exchange. Jackie's words were echoing in Henry's ear, drowning out even the noise of the traffic. She had scored a point and she knew it. She let it sink in quietly. It went deep. Henry was almost trembling.

Jackie rubbed the back of her head and stared at the floor. Meanwhile, Naseau, the family poodle was suffering from heat exposure and panting rapidly on the back seat. Her head must have been pounding.

Jackie had already counted to ten slowly about nine dozen times on this trip. The last thing she wanted was to get into a roaring, screaming match with Henry in this little rolling sauna. So she kept biting her tongue. But the words were definitely coming, even if she was barely holding them in.

To Jackie, the number of false premises that Henry was operating under was astonishing.

To Henry, it was all a numbers game.

There was no way, according to Henry's thinking, that he could get his hands on that kind of money, other than becoming heir to Uncle Clyde's fortune. To him it was all a business proposition. He was investing in Uncle Clyde and anticipating a whopping return on investment. If it meant schlepping over to Uncle Clyde's house in rush hour traffic on a muggy day, well--what road to financial fortune was ever clear sailing? Great rewards exacted a price, and Henry was quite willing to pay any price of transforming himself into a lap dog if the success of the mission required it. Some things were worth the sacrifice. All success had some price.

Jackie, of course, saw the situation somewhat differently. The price that Henry was paying was in fact his very life. A decade of his life had gone by while waiting, and it was not retrievable. Henry couldn't seem to understand that fact. To Jackie, idealist that she was, the notions of enterprise, passion, challenge, overcoming obstacles, sticking to something, putting your heart and soul on the line for what you truly believe, were not outworn Victorian adages. They produced the American dream.

Jackie was a true believer. Maybe Henry should have looked after the kids and she would have proven to him what it really takes to be an entrepreneur. She would have focused. She would have committed. She would have persisted. And she would have succeeded.

What she had tried to make Henry understand was that even if Uncle Clyde died tomorrow and left all his money to his only relative, Henry was still going to be the loser because the price he would have paid was too high.

The fact that Uncle Clyde was showing no indication of leaving this life anytime soon, along with the fact that Henry had no guarantee that he would get any of the money when old man did pass away, only added to the madness of the whole scheme.

But Jackie still said nothing more and the car eventually exited off the expressway. The only relief in sight was from the heat, the fumes and the noise. Only on the outside. They would both still remain hot under the collar, inhaling an atmosphere of disrespect and enduring the painful sounds of their own onerous silence.

Before long they had wound through the circular streets and posh boulevards of Uncle Clyde's ranch villa neighborhood. When they pulled into the driveway, they found him sitting outside on a chaise-lounge with lemonade in hand. Dressed in his boxer shorts and a light t-shirt, he sat like a playful child, well within the turning radius of a garden sprinkler that doused him with a refreshing shower on every revolution. He was having a grand time.

Uncle Clyde looked exuberant but ironically, not nearly as happy as Henry. In the three seconds it took to pull up the driveway, Henry had undergone an amazing transformation. His eyes were sparkling, a huge grin appeared and his back straightened. Without a moment's delay, he bounded out of the car and with all the enthusiasm he could muster, yelled out:

"Hi, Uncle Clyde!"

"O Henry!"

They hugged each other. Jackie joined in.

They were all getting wet.

It was the last time that Henry would get to act in this fashion. Within twenty-four hours, Uncle Clyde came down with a cough, fever and chills. The chills turned to rigors. His breathing became more difficult. He started choking with his cough and became increasingly pale. He had to be taken to the local hospital where he was diagnosed with lobar pneumonia that got progressively worse and he never recovered.

Henry and Jackie both experienced mixed emotions. But what different mixtures they were.

After the funeral, Henry received a call from Uncle Clyde's lawyer and executor of his will. He rushed to their appointment, only to learn that Uncle Clyde had left explicit instructions for the estate.

Fifty percent was to go to the Humane Society. The other half was to be held in trust to be divided equally between Henry's three children upon each attaining the age of twenty-five.

Poor Henry! His dream became a nightmare.

But Jackie began using her imagination … and her passion too! The tables had turned.

* * *

SUCCESS

Dream!
Dream big,
Dream big enough ...
It can come true, if you dare.

Dare!
Dare to be ...
Dare to be great.
'Twill soon appear within your grasp.

Grasp!
Grasp the future,
Grasp the future in faith ...
If you believe, you'll find success.

Success?
All that you can be ...
'Twill all be yours if you take it.

Take it!
Seize it with the heart ...
'Tis passion that makes the future.

The future?
It's now and ever will be
Exactly what you make it.

—A.C.S.

The Compliance Test

Recall that this book is a prescription.
Having read this tale, you may experience some "side effects."
*Take some time now to **describe** any of the possible "side effects" that you observe:*
–Dr. YES!

Inspiration ...

Entertainment ...

Challenge ...

Imagination ...

Breakthrough ...

Self-discovery ...

Crisis ...

Motivation ...

Humor ...

Increased appetite for ... YES!

YOUR PRESCRIPTION

TEN (10) IMAGINATION EXERCISES

If you keep dreaming, "I would like to", but your pie remains in the sky, then use the following exercises for your imagination to add both space and focus to fire your passion.

1. **Close your eyes and travel anywhere.**
2. **Gaze into the sky.**
3. **Sit by the ocean.**
4. **Play with toys.**
5. **Go on a hike.**
6. **Ask an original question.**
7. **Follow science fiction.**
8. **Doodle.**
9. **Act out your favorite character.**
10. **Brainstorm.**

*As you pursue these exercises, you will observe your mind expand and your world enlarge. New mental paradigms will form and a new **goal set** will emerge to prompt you into action.*

–Dr. YES!

6

Billy's Big Break
("But ...")

*'But ...!' There is the inevitable excuse, the irresistible logic
to cause instant paralysis. With this simple verbal hinge,
massive doors of opportunity swing inward and downward
to shut out the inviting possibilities of the future.*

—A.C.S.

Billy awoke, opened his eyes and lifted his head slightly off the beige embroidered pillow. He strained and narrowed his eyes, trying to bring the time display on the VCR into focus.

It was probably some time in the mid-afternoon.

From his comfortably sprawled position, Billy glanced out the window and saw that it was a glorious winter day. The fresh snow covering the ground reflected the bright sunshine in a blinding whiteness. For a moment, he covered his eyes with one hand.

He must have dosed off, lying on the couch in the den, while watching *Geraldo*.

As he was coming to, Billy groggily remembered that

the alarm clock was on the coffee table. He glanced over toward the center of the room. Good, he had not overslept. The alarm had not gone off yet, or did he sleep through it? He was not sure. At last he managed to read the time and it was only two thirty. That meant that he had plenty of time to get to his meeting.

Billy gently eased his head back onto the pillow at the end of the couch. He was living the lifestyle that many unemployed persons enjoy, or else endure.

The alarm clock set-up had been working like a charm, despite his mother's incessant harassing complaints. He wished she would give him a break and get off his case. He blamed her for his attitude, if not his circumstances. She obviously didn't appreciate the real problem.

Three months ago, Billy had missed his regular scheduled meeting and they canceled his benefits immediately. It took him two days and a migraine headache before he got the mess straightened out. It would not happen again.

True, he lived at home. But any twenty-eight year old would have his own necessities and bills. He needed money like everyone else. So now, when his wall calendar reminded him that each Meeting Day had arrived, Billy took no chances. He set his alarm clock and put it on the corner of the coffee table as an insurance policy. Just in case ... for some added protection. What a plan.

Billy stared at the bare ceiling.

He was not looking forward to chatting with Cortez. That was a chore. Billy had liked his last employment counselor, a breezy fellow who loved to hear himself talk. He would sit and talk freely a lot more then. That guy even had a sense of humor, but this Cortez was always taking everything so seriously. He was a listener, always insisting on the details, on piecing together Billy's entire month with a deliberateness that was nerve-wracking.

He also asked a lot of questions, which often forced Billy to come up with implausible lies to evade the general conclusion that Cortez was always trying to make. They were antagonists in conflict, not companions in distress. So Billy blamed Cortez for his lack of any original ideas.

And where did these people dream up these titles?

Yes, Cortez was called a *counselor*! That was a bad word. It reminded Billy of Mrs. Higgins, his high school guidance counselor. A lot of help she had turned out to be. It ought to be old Mrs. Higgins lying here on the couch, Billy thought, living on scraps, trying to eke out an existence on the pitiful sum the government was paying him.

What had he learned from this *guidance* counselor to put him on the right path? How did it come to this? Where was Mrs. Higgins anyway? After all, it was she who had talked him into becoming a millwright in the first place. It had been her idea right from the very beginning. What could she have been thinking?

Unhappily, Billy had learned when he eventually got his diploma, that the chances of finding work as a millwright weren't that much better than finding work as an alchemist. But that was water under the bridge. Lots of water. And it was still flowing.

Billy cursed the memory of his old teacher and blamed her for his own career choice. She had caused his mistake.

Billy was now idly watching a small garden spider crawl across the ceiling light, when suddenly, he heard the garage door creak open.

Great! Just what he needed. His mother had returned early from her shopping trip. Billy's bad luck.

The thought of facing both Cortez and his mother, back-to-back, was enough to make Billy scramble desperately but reluctantly off the couch.

But when he stood up, the sudden posture change made him light headed. He started to stumble awkwardly, listing badly to port and then to starboard. He tried to re-establish vestibular equilibrium as he rushed down the basement steps.

That was Billy's life these days. He was staggering from pillar to post going nowhere. Unemployed. Seeking but never finding. Wrong place or wrong time. Too much experience or too little. Companies were either downsizing or uprooting and going elsewhere.

Surely he was not drunk, the world of business had to be. He was intoxicated not by gravity or by booze, he reasoned, but by volatile markets and variable profits. He blamed both the politicians and the economists.

Billy didn't know exactly how he was going to dodge his mother, but he would crawl out a drain pipe if necessary. If Billy was forced to listen, even one more time, to his mother telling him how difficult it had been for her to find work in the recession of 1972, he was going to stick a coat hanger in the electrical outlet.

The truth was, Billy decided, that his mother was a big part of the reason he was still out of work. She was not cooperating. Hadn't he just last month approached her about an excellent business opportunity?

The whole enterprise was explained to him in a hotel meeting room. If he played his cards right, he could 'effortlessly and unconcernedly stroll the shores of economic prosperity and watch his ship sail in. He could take his rightful place in the upper echelons of the financially independent if he could only muster a measly $5,000 to buy some inventory.' The rest of the way could be presumed.

So he was told, so he believed.

No one had ever explained the Latin proverb '*Caveat emptor*', buyer beware.

Billy had figured his mother would jump at the chance to get him started. So no one was more surprised than he was when his mother turned him down flat.

No debate. No argument. No way.

And now she had the nerve, the audacity, to nag him day and night about being unemployed. It was her fault.

Just as Billy reached the bottom step, he could hear the last few words of a message being left by a familiar voice on his answering machine:

"... So make sure you call me before you make any decisions. I hope you get me before I leave. O.K.? ... Bye."

How had he missed the call? But it was just as well. From the few words he did hear, Billy knew the caller had been his girlfriend, Suzanne. That sexy voice.

In his current frame of mind, he was going to give Suzanne a pass too. The very last thing he needed, in the midst of being double-teamed by both Cortez and his mother, was a half hour lecture on the importance of making a good impression.

That was all his girlfriend ever had to say. Her fashion sense, and her fashion "scents" were her obsessions. She did nothing better than dress to kill, while inflaming the olfactory senses with every new fragrance on the market. The epitome of superficiality, that was Suzanne.

But as long as blame was being handed out, Billy knew that Suzanne had her fair share coming. He was positive that if only Suzanne, with her stone cold heart, had been a touch more supportive, he would now be happily employed. *But* she was always on his case too.

Did they think it was easy pounding the pavement,

trudging from company to company, being turned down a dozen times a day?

Billy's reverie of blame and self-pity was interrupted by the ringing of the upstairs telephone. He heard his mother answer.

"Hi, Aunt Cathy ... it's so wonderful to hear your voice ... "

He couldn't believe his luck this time. That conversation was destined to last at least half an hour. Billy quietly grabbed his jacket and ever so gently turned the knob on the back door.

Made it!

Once outside, he shielded his eyes from the great blinding whiteness. He walked a few unsteady steps. The crunching as his shoes hit the snow on the pavement sounded terribly loud. A rush of cool air made him zip up his jacket. With the unsteadiness of a hiker on a steep mountain path, Billy picked his way carefully through the snow banks until he reached the bus stop.

He felt odd--like a newborn child encountering the cold cruel world for the very first time. He was completely unaware that this little mission was the first time in nine days that he had ventured out of the house.

The bus was quick in coming but it was crowded. Billy could hardly stand despite the handrails. But he made it to the office just the same.

After a thirty minute wait, Cortez called Billy into his office. Far from being annoyed at being made to wait, Billy had used the time to get his story straight. At every meeting Billy needed to come up with the names of over twenty companies or agencies that he had approached for work, in some way or another, during the previous month. One for every working day. It was a fairly big job. Luckily, he was not alone.

In an ironic twist, the legions of unemployed spent time searching out not the companies that were hiring but the ones that weren't. They then traded among themselves the names of people in human resources for the companies not hiring, so that those names could be confidently incorporated into the kind of discussion that Billy was about to have. It was a kind of lashing back, a conspiracy, and it gave people like Billy a feeling of winning, of beating the system.

Billy had become so frustrated that he hardly even scanned the 'help wanted' ads in the local paper. There were job opportunities advertised yes, but that was part of the game. Potential employers could justify their internal promotion schemes. The government could create new economic statistics. The media could sell more papers. The public could neglect the unemployed. Everybody else was in on the conspiracy. Only people like Billy knew what it was like to make ten calls and get no answers, or answering machines, or wrong numbers. And when you finally got through, you would hear 'too late' or 'too soon,' 'too young' or 'too old,' always too something or another. The bottom line was rejection after rejection. That was too much for people like Billy.

Resumé? What resumé? Referrals? Who would give a decent reference? Work history? If you had one, you would not be in this mess. Experience? That's why you were looking for work in the first place. Unemployment is a vicious cycle. Billy was spinning in it. He knew it was not his fault. Was it?

Billy looked at his list for today, written on a crumpled-up piece of yellow foolscap paper.

Cortez finally sat down across from him and Billy started at the top.

"I have been looking ..."

Before they had gone a quarter of the way through, Cortez interrupted him:

"Billy, stop right there. Are you sure you actually spoke to these people?"

"Of course," Billy answered. "I want to find work."

And he meant it too. He would often sing to himself his favorite Dolly Parton hit:

"Working nine to five ... "

Billy was adamant that he wanted to find work. He expended great effort, at times, to find work. He would take anything he could find ... to get work. His mother had made that message very clear.

"When you are healthy and unemployed only one thing matters ... finding work."

Just like she says.

Yet the scenario he built in his mind was far removed from reality. For example, no one would have been more surprised than Billy to learn that every month, hundreds of people in similar situations find new jobs. Billy's grip on employment reality was slowly slipping away, and this was something Cortez instinctively recognized.

Cortez fired a major league fast ball.

"Look Billy ... I have an idea that I want to run by you."

Cortez was looking at him with a smirk. Billy started to squirm. What devious little scheme had Cortez cooked up?

"Here's what I want to do. We have a backlog of paperwork that could dam up the Niagara River. I want to hire you, Billy ... to give you a chance to get back on your feet... to reconnect with the world. The money isn't great, but it's not much different from what you earned at your last job. And I think we can keep you busy for at least a year. What do you say?"

Billy sat there, stunned, waiting for Cortez to fashion the smile of the practical joker. But Cortez was serious. This was the real thing ... a job offer was staring Billy in the face. Could he handle it?

As Billy sat there, he realized that Cortez was waiting. It took him a minute to regain his bearings. That was quite a fastball. Cortez was no amateur. He had carefully planned this. Finally, Billy answered:

"Well, I don't know what to say ... under normal circumstances I would jump at the opportunity ... *BUT* ..."

(Silence)

It dawned on him. He had run out of excuses.

Billy was back to work ...

What's your excuse?

* * *

EXCUSES

One excuse, two excuses,
Three excuses, four.
All excuses are only excuses-
That's for sure, and no more.

"But, you say, I must explain:
There really is a claim ..."
Speak to yourself, for in the main,
You're only playing a game.

Your argument is crystal clear,
It's nothing more than fluff,
For deep within, you sure must know,
No excuse is ever enough ...

Unless you choose to pass the buck
And rationalize it too.
The winner's circle must include
Some others just like you.

—A.C.S.

The Compliance Test

Recall that this book is a prescription.
Having read this tale, you may experience some "side effects."
*Take some time now to **describe** any of the possible "side effects" that you observe:*
–Dr. YES!

Inspiration ...

Entertainment ...

Challenge ...

Imagination ...

Breakthrough ...

Self-discovery ...

Crisis ...

Motivation ...

Humor ...

Increased appetite for ... YES!

YOUR PRESCRIPTION

TEN (10) PERSONAL RIBBONS

*If you find yourself making constant excuse (s), adding "**But...**"
to every noble intention, then unwrap your personal package of
life's best by pulling on the ribbons that bear your name:*

1.   **Take ownership.**
2.   **Start somewhere.**
3.   **Pace yourself.**
4.   **Plead guilty.**
5.   **Start over.**
6.   **Think creatively.**
7.   **Respect yourself.**
8.   **Just listen**
9.   **Give thanks.**
10. **Unwrap life.**

*The gift of opportunity is reserved for those who choose to unwrap
it. You can unfold **TODAY** as a template for all your tomorrows
and choose to do so, right side up. Go for it.*

–Dr. YES!

7

Guess Who's Not Coming To Dinner

("One of these days")

Procrastination can steal your life away,
one delayed appointment at a time.

—A.C.S.

Ellen stepped off the curb, bridling impatiently, ready to hurry across the intersection as soon as the light changed.

She was a fine renaissance woman, dressed smartly in casual grey Moroni slacks and a cable knit maroon sweater. She stood tall and elegant like her dad, a shade over 5'9". Ellen had the kind of glowing face and firm figure that drew admiring glances from bystanders waiting on the corner. She had shoulder length ash blonde hair. But her eyes were what most people remembered about Ellen. They were moist brown pools of innocent intrigue, vague reminders of some unspoken nostalgic regret.

As Ellen stood at the corner, eyeing the passing traffic

with a cool imperious gaze, she looked every inch like the urban aristocrat.

But there is much danger in casting stereotypes.

This was an exceptionally warm Saturday afternoon in late April. It was an ideal day for window shopping along Fifth Avenue. Normally Ellen would have needed no special invitation to spend the afternoon browsing through the world's most glamorous fashion boutiques. Today, however, she was meeting her roommate for dinner at Vivacci's, which gave her just over half an hour to travel the thirteen blocks south to 23rd Street.

This year marked Ellen's seventh year in New York City. For all the doom and gloom talk of urban trenches and race wars, she still experienced a rush of adrenaline, a surge of wild and carefree excitement, whenever she walked briskly along Fifth Avenue.

Ellen was reflecting how good the seething metropolis of New York had been for her career. The Big Apple was working out so much better than anyone who knew her had imagined.

It was certainly going a lot better than her father had projected ...

And just like that, in the fleeting moment of an idle thought about her dad, a dark cloud came over her.

It was amazing that after seven years of voluntary exile from her father's affection, the mere thought of him was still enough to trigger a cold surging rush of bitterness and resentment.

Ellen still vividly remembered the last time they had spoken.

It was a Saturday afternoon not much different from this one. Ellen was nineteen at the time and still living at home.

Her father was a Philadelphia cop, a large unrefined man, rough around the edges, who invariably knew only one way, the hard way. And that really meant his way or no way. For most of her teenage years, some spent first in the Brooklyn Academy and later at Washington High, Ellen and her father had a relationship that could best be described as a truce. They had had their fights.

The last one was different.

On that particular Saturday, Ellen had accepted an invitation from Alex Billows, her boyfriend of ten months, to join him for a sunrise picnic on the banks of the Skukyll River in Philadelphia's Fairmont Park.

Even in the midst of the urban racket that thundered away here in midtown Manhattan, Ellen could still very easily transport herself to that blessed morning. Only Alex could have planned anything quite that charming.

In her picturesque imagination, Ellen could still hear the good morning chirping of the robins and cardinals. The water of the Skukyll was like glass, perfectly reflecting the decorative lights that lit up boathouse row. The sweet fragrance of blossoming lilacs filled the air as Alex poured them both a cup of hot lemon tea from his thermos.

In those days, Alex never went anywhere without his guitar. For two years he had labored to master its strings and now he was a natural John Denver imitation. When breakfast was finished--a sumptuous collection of tropical fruits, fresh oatmeal muffins with strawberry jam and tea--Alex took out his guitar and started strumming. They sat on a quilt close to each other and Alex began serenading Ellen in his soft endearing voice, with every love song and sentimental ballad he could remember. Annie's song became Ellen's that day.

> *"You fill up my senses,*
> *Like a night in the forest,*
> *Like a mountain in spring time,*
> *Like a walk in the rain,*
> *Like a storm in the desert,*
> *Like a sleepy blue ocean,*
> *You fill up my senses,*
> *Come fill me again ..."*

John Denver had expressed Alex's sentiments perfectly. The words and music could not be any more appropriate. Ellen drank them both like wine. She felt full and choked up with tears.

As a young woman of nineteen, Ellen had lived the kind of cloistered life that very often befalls the daughter of a big city cop. Understandably so. Alex had been her first serious boyfriend.

Yet that thought was far from her mind, as they later strolled the bank of the Skukyll, dreamily lost in the passion of young love.

Just past the grandstand, right beside the bronze cast of John Kelly hunched over in his racing shell, Ellen now recalled, Alex got down on one knee and proposed to her.

But why was everything so vivid in her mind today? She could rehearse the same sentiments as if it all happened yesterday.

Ellen whistled as she trudged along at a good clip.

She caught a glance of her reflected image when she passed a large plate glass window of Bonwit Teller. No doubt she herself had changed a lot in seven years. This was a new and different woman. She wondered whether Alex had changed, or whether he still had the same twinkling blue eyes, his clean lines and mischievous grin that had charmed her so completely on that Saturday morning, long ago.

Ellen continued to play back the video in her mind and recalled how she had gazed into the eyes of her teenage boyfriend, perched on one knee. There in the park that glorious day, for one brief rapturous moment there was nothing in the world, in the universe, in the whole of creation, but the two of them, lost in the swirling torrent of complete and perfect love. She remembered thinking that her heart would burst from the explosive love she felt for her new fiancé. But she had to make it official.

"Yes. Of course I will!"

Ellen recalled squealing in answer to Alex's proposal. Her consummate scream had been so loud that a passing biker had stopped to see if she needed assistance.

For the rest of the morning they had walked the park, swept up with grand plans for the future. Alex wanted to move to New York City so he could pursue a career in music. Ellen on the other hand, had just finished her first year of commercial art at Drexel; but there was no better place than New York for an aspiring commercial artist.

So Ellen threw her support wholeheartedly behind that part of the plan. It was only when she was sitting in the front seat of Alex's aging Volkswagen Rabbit on their way home, that Ellen allowed the one tiny dark cloud on the horizon to enter her conscious mind.

"What is my father going to say?"

The more she thought about that question, the more worried she became. Gut feelings told her that the conversation would not go well.

These impressions upon her mind as she hustled the last few blocks of her trek today were so real, so detailed. She could recall the minutiae of those life-changing events. She could not arrest the nostalgia, especially when it came to her father.

She remembered when she got home that day, how her father did not disappoint her. He was furious. He could not imagine a teenage bride. Huge mistake.

The first thing he did was to throw Alex out of the house. Ellen tried to leave with him, but her father physically restrained her, preventing her from going anywhere. She ended up in her room, heart broken, tears flowing and fists flailing.

Her father eventually came up and sat on the edge of the bed. He went so far as to apologize for physically restraining her.

Ellen said nothing.

An hour after that, he came back and sat on the edge of the bed again; he spent close to two hours telling her why she couldn't marry Alex. Through her tears Ellen listened, although she still said nothing. Yet every time her father mentioned one of Alex's shortcomings, she felt another tiny stab of pain in her heart. Why couldn't her father just leave her alone?

The saga continued.

The next morning at dawn, Ellen jumped into a cab with suitcases packed and left her father's home, for good.

She had never returned.

There were a few perfunctory exchanges on the telephone when Ellen attempted to call her mother and her father happened to answer the call. But they hadn't spoken as such for seven years.

Ellen was making a quick pace along the busy city streets but she had to stop for another red light. She was going to be late, unless she picked up the pace even more. This was great exercise.

"Why was my father so abrasive and pigheaded?"

She pounded her feet into the pavement as she hurried along, in disgust at the very thought.

She and Alex were married in New York City, in a little side chapel at St. Anselm's. Neither of their families attended the wedding. The first year of the marriage was straight out of a fairytale, save for the behavior of the bride's family.

But an odd and highly disturbing pattern began to emerge in the second year. Alex started to travel a lot, and when he was home, he was distant and aloof. The domestic routines of maintaining a modest one bedroom apartment up in the Village was alien to Alex and so he left that to Ellen. Breakfast in bed and walks in the park soon became a thing of the past, and Ellen began to feel that she was becoming invisible.

Ellen was at a loss to explain the change in Alex and he himself was tight lipped.

Things got worse and eventually, nineteen months after exchanging their vows at St. Anselm's, Alex walked out of the marriage. All he could offer Ellen by way of an explanation was that he needed more air and mountains, more green grass and clear lakes. Why he needed them apart from Ellen he could not say.

To say that Ellen was devastated when Alex ran off was a gross understatement.

The next twelve months were hellish. What made it worse was that her father had been absolutely right about Alex. He had gruesomely predicted the entire scenario. Whatever cop radar he had used to pick up the ugly vibrations from Alex had been right on the mark. That's what made it so hard for her to go home.

Ellen's obvious disappointment was deep. Her emotional pain went even deeper but there was no fathoming her pride. She was in a bottomless pit.

But when her father received the news, that Alex had fled the marriage, he had extended his hand to Ellen in the form of a three page handwritten letter that was as heartfelt as her father had the capacity to be. Ellen had read that letter over and over again.

But it was too late.

Her father had destroyed something in her on that fateful Saturday afternoon that neither time nor sentiment could heal.

Although he had been right about Alex, he had been dead wrong about Ellen and New York City. She had thrived in New York, and at the still tender age of twenty-six she was Assistant Art Director in a small but flourishing Madison Avenue advertising partnership.

So ... take that ... father!

In fact, Ellen still felt a perverse twinge of pride whenever she relayed a piece of news to her father, through her mother, about her latest professional coup.

Yet, as so often happens to men in law enforcement, age had mellowed her father. When Ellen read the birthday cards that he religiously sent, she noticed that they had a softness and tenderness that was endearing. Her father, desperate to re-unite with his only daughter had resorted to sending her little gifts. She received roses one month; Swiss chocolates the next month; mittens the following month.

Why all this was not wearing her down was a mystery to the people who knew Ellen. But she knew that there was a deadness deep inside her when it came to her father that no amount of flowers and confections could resurrect. Ellen called it deadness; her mother called it stubborn pride.

Call it what you will, Ellen was working things out in her own time, if you please. She wouldn't be surprised if one day there was a reconciliation of some kind between the two of them, but Ellen didn't expect it anytime soon. Clearly it was going to take time, and if her father didn't like it, well, he should have thought about that before destroying the psyche of a nineteen year old girl.

It has been said that 'time does heal all wounds' but some take a long, long time. And you cannot hurry it along. Ellen knew that. All she could muster under her breath, were four famous little words.

'One of these days ...'

She was struggling but she now at least had good intentions.

With a slight mist of perspiration on her forehead and a healthy glow on her cheeks, Ellen arrived at Vivacci's. Her roommate Carol was standing inside the door, fidgeting nervously.

"Sorry I'm late, Carol ... how long have you been waiting?"

Ellen waved her hand toward the dining area of the restaurant, leading them to the hostess' podium.

"Ellen, you got an urgent message on the answering machine ... it's about your *father*." Carol said it without looking at Ellen.

"I was just thinking about my father, as a matter of fact. What has he cooked up this time?" Ellen asked carelessly, not bothering to stop.

"It's not from your father, it's *about* your father ... Ellen, he had a stroke. I think you had better look at this."

"Stroke?"

Ellen froze when she heard the word.

Stroke!

She grabbed the piece of paper from Carol. It was true. Her father was in grave condition at Mercy Hospital after suffering a massive stroke at two o'clock that afternoon. The prognosis was poor. Finally, the message said to return home as quickly as possible.

Ellen re-read the message twice. It was really true. Her face looked ashen and her hands trembled with the note.

She looked at Carol who was looking away.

She felt a tear trickle down her warm cheek.

Ellen buried her head in her hands. Waves of emotion were rising within and flooding the shores of her soul. She could feel the gusts of a tropical storm raging in her bosom.

Then, time stood still for a moment, all was lost and she became numb. She could not think.

She threw her arms around Carol and began to weep as if to purge her spirit. Her love for her father erupted like Mount St. Helen's volcano. Suddenly, she wanted him more than anything else. She wanted to look into his eyes and see him smile even but once with her. She wanted to kiss the hand that wrote those letters and to cradle his head upon her lap.

Carol reminded her she was still in New York.

"Hurry Ellen, get a cab. You don't have much time. It might be quicker to drive than to fly, but call American anyway, just to be sure--they have a shuttle."

Ellen hugged and squeezed Carol some more. They kissed and without another word, Ellen rushed through the restaurant's revolving door.

A line of taxis was parked outside the door. Thank heaven for small mercies. Ellen jumped into the first car and shouted at the driver:

"Please, I'm going uptown, and I'll tell you exactly where in a minute. But hurry ... move it!"

As the car weaved into the busy traffic, Ellen looked at the note and read it for the umpteenth time. They had given the number of the Mercy Hospital for her to call.

She pulled out her cellular phone and took three deep breaths. She dialed the number and asked to be put through to the ICU.

When she got through, she identified herself and asked for the doctor in charge. When the doctor came on the telephone he said a few brief words to her.

It took just a second or two to sink in. Then as the taxi maneuvered along Fifth Avenue, Ellen suddenly exploded and started screaming:

"No ... No ... Dear God, no ... Please ...

"Oh no ... Noooooooooo."

Too late.

Perhaps *one of these days* she'll come to. And then again, perhaps never.

* * *

PROCRASTINATION

Put it off until a later date,

Reduce the stress for now.

Other times will be ideal

'Cause I might by then know how.

Ridiculous it seems to be,

Always in such a big hurry --

Since there is a lot more time

To tap each opportunity ... NO!

If you were sure of tomorrow,

No one would even care, but

A better time there'll never be,

The time is now, the place is here.

I'd seize this chance, avoid the sorrow.

Only presume today is yours, and

Never put off 'till tomorrow.

—A.C.S.

The Compliance Test

Recall that this book is a prescription.
Having read this tale, you may experience some "side effects."
*Take some time now to **describe** any of the possible "side effects" that you observe:*
–Dr. YES!

Inspiration ...

Entertainment ...

Challenge ...

Imagination ...

Breakthrough ...

Self-discovery ...

Crisis ...

Motivation ...

Humor ...

Increased appetite for ... YES!

YOUR PRESCRIPTION

TEN (10) MINUTES TO MIDNIGHT

The procrastinator is given to putting off everything to the last minute. He can suspend life by choosing to wait for **'one of these days'**. *As the clock keeps ticking away, you can trace his degeneracy as he slips into midnight with increasing desperation.*

10.	**"I have lots of time."**
9.	**"The race is not to the swift."**
8.	**"It's just not that important."**
7.	**"I always pull it off."**
6.	**"I have too much else to do."**
5.	**"I'll do it soon."**
4.	**"That will do."**
3.	**"It will go away."**
2.	**"Somebody, help me."**
1.	**"I don't care any more ..." Midnight.**

But procrastination is a habit, a pattern of behavior, and one that can be changed. Awareness of the potential consequences can go a long way to cultivating a renewed **sense of urgency**. *It implores you to harness the resources of the ever-present moment and to respond to challenge and opportunity with "warm intensity".*

–Dr. YES!

8

Lord Of The Manor

("Perhaps")

You will never know what is possible for you
until you know what is most desirable.

−A.C.S.

Life is dispensed but one day at a time. Any given day in a life can make all the difference. The most important days of our lives often come unannounced. No fanfare. A normal dawn gives rise to a typical sunrise and then the day unfolds. Which way? Who knows ...

That's how it was for the Thompsons. They started out the day in such a grand mood, almost tipsy, full of high-spirited camaraderie, ready to embark on the high adventure of their first house hunting experience. They were excited but also quite nervous.

Jenny had finally convinced Grant that their time had come. It was now time to be rid of cranky landlords, time enough to crawl out of the tenant mentality of no maintenance living. She persuaded him that it was indeed time to latch on to the middle class dream of owning your own home, your own little plot of God's green earth, with your own roof over your head.

Surely it was time to stake out a tiny corner of the world that they could call their own.

Jenny had been ready for years. Grant, however, had been a hard sell. It had not exactly taken a stick of dynamite to get him moving, but almost.

Of course Jenny knew that Grant could be indecisive. She had waited four years for him to propose. And it had taken another two years of nudging to get him to set a wedding date.

Grant Thompson was the kind of man who couldn't decide what section of the newspaper to read first without pausing to "think it through".

Think it through!

It was his mantra. Jenny heard that evil phrase a dozen times a week.

Well, Grant had certainly taken his sweet time thinking through home ownership. But the more he learned, the more he was convinced that it did make sense to take the plunge.

In periods of economic growth, especially with high inflation, a principal residence is a protected investment. Historically, it was the best. Decades of numbers were there to prove that. Then there are the sheltered capital gains, the mortgage interest deductibility, the collateral credit power line advantage, the pride of ownership, the stability and the security for the family.

All this and more Grant had come to appreciate. So he had analyzed mortgage tables, listened to negotiation tapes, played with financing software, and ploughed through so many demographic analyses that Jenny couldn't stand it anymore.

How many other men, Jenny wondered, felt a need to thoroughly understand the monetary effects of sixty-year Elliot Wave Cycles on inverted mortgage yield curves, before they'd even consider talking to a real estate agent?

Oh ... it had been a torturous ordeal for Jenny all right, but perseverance had won out in the end. Grant had come on side. They were ready to go. They were armed to do battle.

Anticipating that Grant would eventually succumb to either logic or just sweet wifely pressure, Jenny had gone ahead and tracked down a real estate agent ahead of time. She found a fellow named Al Luddon, the twin brother of a woman with whom Jenny shared her office.

Al was extremely helpful. He had arranged for them to see five houses on the first day, all of them chosen according to a careful weighting scheme that Grant had dreamed up.

The first appointment was scheduled for nine-thirty on Saturday morning.

Now that the morning had arrived, Jenny stood in front of the stove in her floral cotton housecoat, flipping blueberry pancakes on the grill, singing and giggling like a schoolgirl.

In his own way, Grant had joined in the excitement. He was relaxed and unusually talkative. He smiled broadly as he entertained the family with grand plans of what he was going to do as Lord of the new Manor.

The children--fourteen year old Sue and her thirteen year old brother David--were a little less enthusiastic. First, after being witness to endless discussions, debates, and teary-eyed demands, they could hardly believe that their father would ever go through with it. More importantly, with all their lifelong friends living in the current neighborhood, they had no real desire to move to a new one.

But even these teenagers, despite the prospect of leaving their friends behind, started coming around, caught up in the enthusiasm of a suddenly chatty father and a giddy singing mother.

That was how the day had begun.

The first house Al took them to see was a bland, box-like structure that looked uninspiring.

Jenny was not unduly worried. It was not as if Grant was going to buy the first house he looked at anyway. If there were a few undesirable homes on the list, better to get them out of the way early.

Besides, how can you spot a great house and a good deal unless you first look at a couple of houses that are much less so?

Even Grant had taken it in stride, offering nothing more than a few non-committal grunts when Al Luddon had asked him what he thought of the house.

After that brief visit, they drove over to the second house on the list which was less than five minutes away.

When Grant pulled up the car in front of the second house, Jenny figured that Al must have written the address down wrong, or at least she fervently hoped that was the case. On seeing the house, Grant looked over sharply at Jenny who managed to look away.

"Is this some kind of joke?"

They got out of their Plymouth Caravan.

Al was already out of his car, waiting for them on the front walkway. He looked at the house with curiosity, his eyes darting around the property as if seeing it for the first time.

The three of them walked silently up the path together toward the front door.

This was a Cape Cod style home that had a carport on one side and an ancient TV antenna on the other. The antenna was tilting badly towards the front of the house. Wispy tufts of crab grass had sprouted up between the cracks in the walkway and the lawn was an overgrown mess.

On the front verandah which was painted in thick coats of battleship gray, sat a rusty, old car seat assembly, apparently from the front seat of a '73 Ford Fury.

What masochistic impulse had crept into Al's brain, Jenny wondered? Why after all the advance warning about Grant's neat and orderly mind, had Al decided to include this "little gem" on the itinerary?

They started walking up the steps to the front door.

When they reached the top, Jenny noticed a gray nest or hive of some sort tangled up in leaves and brush, wedged in the far corner of the verandah overhang.

With an unhappy premonition Jenny edged closer to the nest to try to get a better look.

"A-a-a-a-h …!"

Although not a nervous woman by disposition, Jenny let out a startled cry when she suddenly saw a handful of wasps buzzing in and around the nest.

She ran down the front steps and once Grant had appraised the situation, he quickly followed her.

Al walked down and joined them.

Frustrated, Jenny could feel five years of intense house lobbying slowly starting to slip away.

Grant wasn't looking at the house anymore. He had turned to the street. He was staring out at the subdivision with complete fascination, totally absorbed in the surrounding landscape, like a wayward urban planning student who had accidentally stumbled into the forbidden city.

Jenny knew the technique well. Grant was emotionally withdrawing. If she wanted to salvage something from this excursion, then she had better get some answers.

Al preempted her.

"I know that this house may not look that great, but you--"

Jenny interrupted him, desperately trying to control her fury.

"No, it doesn't look great, Al. It looks horrible. It looks very unlike the kind of houses that we asked you to show us."

Grant stood there mute, transfixed with the architectural wonders of the detached brick homes not far away.

Al collected himself and using all the professional polish he could muster, he answered Jenny in an excessively polite and formal tone.

"From the criteria you sent me I concluded that you were sophisticated buyers who could appreciate value. While this house is a mess, it is also the best value I have in the entire book of current listings in the area. The selling price that we have yet to discuss, reflects that value. But I think there is room to negotiate a steal on this one."

The word 'sophisticated' had caught Grant's ear. He turned to listen more intently. Meanwhile, Jenny whispered to herself.

"Beautiful answer, Al. Nice comeback."

Grant looked at Jenny with a hint of suspicion in his eyes. She responded with understanding and warmth.

"Well Al, that was thoughtful, it really was. And who knows, maybe we will eventually want to take a closer look at this place, but the day is short and the hour is long. Where is the third house on the list? What's next?"

Grant was eyeing both of them with a look that school teachers reserve for children who have just subjected them to a feeble practical joke that didn't work. But he relented and without saying a word, he followed Jenny to the car.

Grant and Jenny drove in silence to the next house. After a short walk through it, with Al highlighting the finished recreation room, the aluminum siding, and the forced air furnace, they left just as quickly as they came.

Another disappointment.

Had something gone wrong somewhere?   Poor communication? Was it Al's poor judgment?

The fourth house was no better.

Jenny, in spite of herself, was now frustrated and ready to go home. At this point, talking had ceased. Silence filled the air as they stood uneasily on the sidewalk, like pallbearers who are told to wait at the bottom of the church stairs for the bagpiper to finish so they can do the essentials and start to roll.

Jenny reflected on fate and why it had so cruelly conspired against her in the all-decisive moment.

Al was past suggesting anything.

But strangely enough, it was Grant who had urged them to press on. They had formulated a schedule and so what if the day had been a total waste? That was no justification for letting the schedule hang. And Grant, being Grant, insisted that they finish what they had begun. He had taken control of the agenda. At least he thought so.

Al led the way in his eight year old Mazda RX-7. The drive to the last house took a good twenty minutes and the conversation in the Dodge Caravan was all about dinner plans, tax deadlines and dental appointments. Buying a house did not even come up.

Jenny sighed, reassuring herself that one lost battle does not necessarily mean defeat in the war. She would live to fight again another day.

The Mazda pulled into a gravel circular driveway and the Caravan followed suit.

Jenny jumped out of the car.

"Well, what have we here ... very interesting!"

The setting sun bathed the next house in an almost supernatural radiant glow. There was a mature Maple tree in the front of the house but the lawn was still handsomely manicured, evidenced by the tiny hand-dug irrigation furrows that surrounded the entire perimeter of the lawn.

The house itself was Dutch Colonial, set off elegantly with muted pastel trim. The front door was a wide, solid oak, hand-carved masterpiece. Inside, the front hallway was covered with deep green marble tile from Italy that gave the vestibule a touch of elegant warmth and grace. There was a floating staircase leading to a balcony above. Eye-catching.

Jenny couldn't wait for Al or Grant, she took off on her own, straight to the kitchen. It was twice the size of her current kitchen. One of the walls was done in original fieldstone, although the fireplace had been replaced with a wood burning stove. The Gleedale cupboards and the island in the middle were made of oak, and the floor was covered with beautifully decorated, square ceramic tiles.

"Unbelievable!"

Jenny could not imagine that this house was in their price range, but she was enjoying the tour anyway. The living room and the bedroom produced more 'oohs' and 'aahs,' and finally Jenny went to look for Al and Grant. They were standing on the back patio.

"This couldn't possibly be in our price range ... could it?"

"No," Al answered, "the asking price is $11,000 more than your upper limit, but I wanted you to see that there are nice houses to buy, if we take the time to look."

Jenny looked over at Grant, who looked like a chess player three moves away from being checkmated and with no idea how to escape.

"Come on, Grant," she pleaded, "surely you agree ... is this not a fabulous house?"

"That it is."

The house did suit their needs. It was small enough to be cozy but big enough to be comfortable. The area was quiet. There were young families on the same street. Almost all the amenities they would need were within walking distance. Even the local school. Access to a major artery was no problem so they could easily commute to work.

Late that night, they were caught up in the real chess game. Real estate *poker* may be better. In any case, they had been over it again and again. But Grant was not budging.

He and Jenny were sitting at their kitchen table with a counter offer spread before them. After a temper tantrum, a gourmet meal and the most compelling logical argument that Jenny could mount, she had convinced Grant that they had to make another offer.

They had chopped $9,000 off the asking price and put in a condition that the seller pay for the land survey. The seller had come back with an offer that indicated they would accept $5,000 less than the asking price, but they required the Thompsons to cover the survey.

To Jenny, who was trying her utmost to remain

composed, it was a lay-up, a gimme. She was all for signing the counter offer and sending it back immediately.

But Grant thought that they were leaving too much on the table.

"Curse those negotiation tapes!" Jenny mumbled to herself.

Grant wanted to wait it out.

Jenny was frantic. Over the space of two hours of intense discussion with Grant, she had established several facts. He agreed that it was a great house. He agreed that it was probably better than anything else they were likely to see. He agreed that he wanted to own it. He agreed that it probably wouldn't last that long.

Jenny was left grasping at straws. If he agreed with her on all the major points, why was he still so stubbornly refusing to accept the counter offer?

Jenny studied Grant. She could see that he was upset. But why? She instinctively knew the answer ... he had no logical reasons for refusing to sign. He just could not bring himself to make a decision of this magnitude.

"It's okay, Grant," she said gently in a whisper. "Just sign the paper. It's no big deal. We can sell it next week if we don't want to keep it. Let's just sign it. Sometimes, Grant ... you just have to decide."

The telephone interrupted her, and when Jenny put the receiver to her ear she discovered it was Al.

Bad news. Another buyer had surfaced. By law, all offers had to be presented.

"If you want the house, you'd better act fast." That was the warning Al left her with.

When Jenny told Grant, he told her that it was just an old negotiation technique and nothing to worry about. And there they sat, in a most painful impasse.

Jenny almost felt sorry for Grant. He was trapped in some kind of self-imposed block of ice, completely unable to move or act.

But Jenny wanted the house ... desperately! She tried one more time to build a little fire under the future Lord of the Manor.

"I'll get another part-time job if I have to. I will work on my parents for some help with the downpayment. If we manage another five or six thousand down, the carrying cost will be more than manageable. I know we can handle this."

"That's not the point."

"But what is?"

"Is this the house to buy at this price? Should we be looking around some more?"

"But you already said how much you really like this house. I like it. I love it. The kids love it. It is exactly what we need."

"That's not the point." Grant had no point of his own but he kept stalling.

They kept circling and circling but got no closer to a decision. Finally, at eleven forty-five they decided to decide in the morning.

Later Jenny was in bed when she heard the telephone ring. She strained to hear the answering machine which was barely above a whisper. A little adrenal shock went through her system.

It was Al.

"Sorry folks ... I hate to tell you this, but the house just so--."

"Oh ... no!"

Jenny rolled over and hugged the covers to her neck, as the tears streamed down her cheeks on to the huge feather pillow.

They came close but not close enough.

In the morning Grant was no better, no clearer and no more prepared to act. He rationalized that maybe that house was not *the* Manor after all.

"If you hold to things lightly, then whatever blows away could not have been yours in the first place."

What a ridiculous conclusion to draw, after the fact.

Deep down Grant knew it, so he would try to make it up. He owed it to Jenny to at least try again. Perhaps they should talk to Al further about the old house that might appeal to 'sophisticated buyers' who could perceive genuine value for money.

They talked. They revisited the old place. They

talked some more. The children got in on the act. They drove out there in the daytime to have a careful look at the neighborhood. They went back for a night time perspective.

Jenny had a friend, Gill Walker, who specialized in renovations and additions. He was ecstatic. He saw the possibilities and shared them freely.

Jenny got excited again.

Grant vacillated some more.

It was little David who broke through the block of ice.

"Daddy, if I were a man, I would not live on the edge of a fence. It is a dangerous place. It must hurt up there. I would get off ... "

"David, this is a big decision for big people."

"You remember how I learned to swim?" David fired back. "My friend Ron pushed me into the water one day at the YMCA camp. I was only nine. I was not afraid, I just swam. That's why you still have not learned to swim yourself. Nobody ever pushed you. Now everybody is trying to help you with a push."

"Help me?"

Grant was still very much in denial. His son David was turning up the heat.

"Daddy, listen. Listen to mummy. Listen to Mr. Luddon. Listen to Mr. Walker. And if you can't hear what they are saying, then listen to me. Jump down off the fence, daddy. At least if you land on the wrong side you will know, then you will get up and go over to the right one. And then you'll be there. Instead of being nowhere."

The silent pause was pregnant ...

It gave birth.

Grant hugged young David as he melted.   Jenny reached over and kissed them both.

"Now you *are* the Lord of the Manor."

She was very happy. They were all very happy.

* * *

CHOICE

This or that?
Here or there?
Now or then ...?
Whenever.

It's a pain nevertheless --
The pain of choosing.
What seems like a privilege,
When it becomes real
Personal or private ...
Whoever.

That lonely privilege
Becomes a pain.
But that's the price
Of the ultimate pleasure.
Pleasure or else ...
Whatever.

When 'tis done, 'tis done
You're overwhelmed with pride --
The pride of having made
By nature or nurture,
A real though difficult choice ...
Forever.

—A.C.S.

The Compliance Test

Recall that this book is a prescription.
Having read this tale, you may experience some "side effects."
*Take some time now to **describe** any of the possible "side effects" that you observe:*
–Dr. YES!

Inspiration ...

Entertainment ...

Challenge ...

Imagination ...

Breakthrough ...

Self-discovery ...

Crisis ...

Motivation ...

Humor ...

Increased appetite for ... YES!

YOUR PRESCRIPTION

TEN (10) DRY BONES

In the valley of indecision where every opportunity is answered with the apprehension and uncertainty of "Perhaps", look around for the dry bones that carry a warning message. They provide clues to get you out of the valley and to avoid it in future:

1. **No passion**
2. **Incomplete information**
3. **Double-mindedness**
4. **Excessive advice**
5. **Conflicting values**
6. **Insecurity**
7. **Superstition**
8. **Inadequate resources**
9. **Overcaution**
10. **No sense of responsibility**

*As you make connections between these relics of what could have been, you will regain the awareness and control to make you **become more decisive.** Then, as you decide, these bones will be covered with sinews and flesh and skin, and you will start to live again, like a mighty warrior upon your feet.*

–Dr. YES!

9

Nothing But Net

("I really want to")

*Caution is advisable before we stop,
NOT before we start.*

—A.C.S.

High school days were fun, arguably the best ...

Riiinnnnnggggg! The 3:25 dismissal bell clanged through the hallways. Another day was over at George Washington High, which was fine by Mark Brel. For the last eighty-five minutes Mark had been cooped up in history class.

He hurried over to his locker and then hustled down to the gym to avoid the bulging eyes and popping neck veins of his basketball coach, Mr. Edwards. Make no mistake, practice started at 3:45 sharp everyday and life was sweeter when you got there on time.

It was not that Mark needed any special prompting. B-ball practice was the highlight of his day. Mark loved the feeling of 'going to the hole', of blowing by the defenders, or sometimes laying back for the drop pass to toss up three pointers. He even reveled in just playing good defense.

He enjoyed working himself into a hot sweat. He loved it so much that when practice was over he would linger on the court, inventing new slamorama moves, tossing free throws, playing '21', or just working on his trick shots.

With a basketball in his hands, Mark felt a freedom to be himself that was unique in his limited experience. At home he had to lie low, brokering the battles and ground wars that his parents waged practically every night of the week. And in class, there were so many bright lights running around, blurting out the correct answers before he even knew what the questions were, that he never stood a chance.

But with basketball in hand, all that changed.

On the basketball court Mark was transformed. There was no more of that holding back, that social awkwardness, or shyness around girls, or that general hesitation and concealment that Mark experienced in new situations. All these heavy laments of leaving childhood behind and moving forward along the dark burdensome road to adulthood, dissolved into nothing when he was dribbling the basketball with confidence and smooth athletic grace, with sweat drenching his body and his breathing deep and regular.

Today Mark was feeling good. He was on his game these days and had had a fine work out. He could not get enough. Last game he was eight for thirteen from the field and four of six from the line, with seven rebounds. Not bad.

But formal practice had been tough this afternoon. Coach Edwards had detected some cockiness in the team and he wanted to run it out of them. They had hardly touched the ball during the whole practice. After putting them through a long series of intense wind sprints, crab drills, board touches and break downs, Coach Edwards called for an eight minute controlled scrimmage and then, that was it. He sent them home.

But Mark was not satisfied. So he grabbed a ball from the rack and walked out on to the court.

Mark began his extra practice by trying to remedy a flaw in his fade away jump shot that his father had pointed out to him after the last game. Apparently he was cocking his head to the right just before he released the ball. Mark threw up a dozen jumpers in a row to see if he could work it out.

Tiring of that, he settled into a rhythmic pattern of randomly shooting baskets from all over the floor. Then he worked on left hand pivots and finally right hand pivots. Then he spent some time on lay ups, all the while moving in a casual unhurried pace.

Getting restless, he looked around the gym. Maybe there was someone around he could coax into a game of '21'.

In the far corner, he watched some freshmen in black socks and cut-off blue jeans playing some crazy game of 4-square that culminated in a free throw.

No luck. No real interest there. The gym was almost empty.

Then Mark looked in the other far corner, and he noticed a couple of female students leaning against the wall, with their heads tilted together in the giggling conspiratorial fashion of teenage girls.

One of the girls he recognized. She was Irene Galat from his history class. The other one he did not know.

Now Mark was good enough friends with Irene that had he wanted to, he could have walked right over and joined the conversation. But the thought alone made his throat go dry. Besides, maybe they were in the middle of something earth shattering or just intensely personal.

So Mark bounced the ball once more and then sent up a long lazy floater from the free throw line that swished through the net without touching the rim.

Nothing but net.

He retrieved the ball. But then his attention became divided between the round piece of leather in his hands and the mysterious brunette in the corner. She was cute.

He dribbled in that direction.

For the thousandth time Mark cursed his painful and terminal shyness. It was a debilitating shyness that seemed to be getting worse, not better. The voice of reason, trying to help, whispered in his ear:

"Go over and say hello. It won't kill you."

Maybe, thought Mark, it is just that easy. But a second voice of unreason, louder and more demanding than the first, put a stop to it.

"Forget it ... why make a fool of yourself? Stay where you are."

And so there he was, stuck in the middle of the floor with two voices double tracking like crazy in his head.

It was the same old story. When Mark met new people in new situations he would start to feel his cheeks getting warm and his eyes would drift downward. His words would get backed up to the point where he had to start each one five or six times before it came out whole.

Why put himself through it?

No wonder then, as a rule, Mark held to his own counsel and hung back. He would let the schemers and the backslappers of the world light up the social skies. But he had to admit to himself that the brunette was charming. She also looked vaguely familiar.

Mark racked his brain trying to remember where he had come across that short pixie haircut and what could be soft, dreamy eyes.

He tried not to stare but he nonchalantly switched to a side basket that was closer to the two girls.

At first he thought they were oblivious to his presence, but looking out of the corner of his eye he could see them cutting side glances his way.

Mark got a better look at the brunette. She was tall and athletic but economical in her movements, and she had a broad, expansive, and highly appealing laugh. He knew her from somewhere.

As he continued to dribble and shoot baskets and polish his bag of tricks, it became obvious to Mark that *he* was the only reason they were there. If there was any conspiratorial giggling going on, it was ultimately directed at him.

Finally it struck him. He even remembered her name. Bonnie Brannigan. *Déja vu.*

Bonnie and Irene were cousins, and if Mark remembered the story correctly, Bonnie went to St. Matthew's which was just across the river.

He had met her at a pig roast at Irene's place last summer. In fact, they had been opponents in a hotly contested game of lawn darts that Bonnie's team had eventually won.

Mark remembered how intrigued he had been by Bonnie's free and easy manner, and her deadly aim. The group of coeds had spent forty minutes chatting beside the tool shed.

Mark started to smile as he bounced the basketball. It was all coming back to him ...

That night had finished with a group of them going to the ice cream stand, and then they went down to the river to escape the summer heat.

Mark remembered sitting on the bank, enjoying the cool breeze. Although he hadn't spoken directly to Bonnie, he had been acutely aware of her presence. She really did have an infectious charm, gentle but playfully high-spirited.

Now here she was in his gymnasium, forty minutes

after basketball practice had finished, coyly leaning against the wall, waiting for him to crawl out of his shell long enough to say 'hello'.

How long did a girl have to wait?

Mark had every intention of marching right over there and saying 'hello', but he couldn't move. His locomotor apparatus was obviously taking orders from some mysterious agent other than his cortex.

He glanced over again and Bonnie almost caught his eye.

This was silly... or more precisely... it was quite sad. Mark was in the grip of a tormented shyness that engulfed his will, his sentiments, his best wishes and his fondest desires. The more he thought of her smooth creamy skin, her smokey eyes and her small child-like hands, the more tormenting the shyness became.

This was getting ridiculous. What was it going to take?

Mark stood underneath the basket and practiced an underhanded alley oop pass.

The girls were looking restless and Mark figured they would soon leave. He thought about what he might say if he did approach them.

But why did it matter? No judges were standing by, ready to flash a scorecard that would mark him on verbal proficiency.

The key was to act fast. Mark thought of something his grandmother liked to tell him:

"Mark, when you're a teenager, you spend weeks and months of your life agonizing over what people think of you. When you turn forty, life gets easier and you take up a new resolve ... you wouldn't give a rat's pajamas for what other people think of you. Period. But it isn't until you turn sixty that you finally realize the truth: People aren't thinking about you at all. Remember that, son."

For some strange reason, that idea comforted Mark. Whether he said something or not, whether he sounded intelligent or scatterbrained, in the long run it was immaterial. The world would go on pretty much the way it always had.

The only thing he might lose, if he didn't go over and say 'hi', was the chance (just maybe!) of holding Bonnie's innocent hands in his.

He might lose the opportunity (let's hope!) to hear that boisterous laugh, or to listen to Bonnie tell stories about visiting Disney World, or to watch her lay in the grass and stare at the moon, wishing on a falling star. He would be the one missing it, no one else. The loss would be his and his alone.

That reality bothered Mark.

The world was full of shy people and the truth was ... the world couldn't care less about shyness and the people who have it. It just went on like wheels within wheels in the circle of life, shyness or no shyness.

But the shyness that Mark experienced was holding *him* back. Of that much he was sure. He had to overcome the problem.

Mark could see that untamed shyness would always hurt him, no matter what else he decided to do with his life. Somewhere it had to stop.

He watched the girls collect their knapsacks as they walked towards the door.

It was now or never.

Mark bit the inside of his lip so hard it almost bled.

Finally he called out:

"Bonnie Brannigan? Is that you?"

"You did remember ... I told you he would remember, Irene."

Bonnie spun around.

Mark was nervous and he could feel the customary dryness in the back of his throat. He had to fight to look at her rather than the floor.

But when he looked at Bonnie, he could sense his reward for having taken the chance. She was looking him straight in the eye with a bursting smile on her face.

What laser beams!

She cocked her head to one side and with a sudden attack of shyness of her own, she gave Mark a wink.

"It is so nice to see you again ... Mark."

"Thanks, Bonnie. You look great. Thanks for coming over. How are things at St. Matt's?"

Mark couldn't believe how easily the words were flowing. He walked over to the two of them. Bonnie was still smiling. With the tiny adorable hands that Mark loved so much, she tenderly grabbed his shoulder and kissed him on the cheek.

The basketball rolled aimlessly away.

Bonnie was humming as she slowly leaned away, with her eyes riveted on Mark's lips as if she were absorbing a high energy radiation that made her melt in those moments. She was singing inside:

"Did you ever know that you're my hero
You're everything I wish I could be,
I can fly higher than an eagle,
'Cause you are the wind beneath my wings."

Mark had just found a new challenge and he got nothing but net on this, his first true roll-up. He thought to himself, perhaps Michael Jordan's are not born, they are made.

* * *

SHY

Shy?
What is your life if you hesitate ...

To break the ice
To dare to ask

To step on stage
To take a bow

To make the first move
To volunteer

To stand your guard
To defend a right

To come on strong
To stare down the opposition

To be seen or heard
To know or be known

To take a chance
On YOU?

Shy?
A mere shadow of what could have been.

—A.C.S.

The Compliance Test

Recall that this book is a prescription.
Having read this tale, you may experience some "side effects."
*Take some time now to **describe** any of the possible "side effects" that you observe:*

–Dr. YES!

Inspiration ...

Entertainment ...

Challenge ...

Imagination ...

Breakthrough ...

Self-discovery ...

Crisis ...

Motivation ...

Humor ...

Increased appetite for ... YES!

YOUR PRESCRIPTION

TEN(10) BODY LANGUAGE SIGNS

*You may be the person who knows that you really want to have, to do and to be the best that you can.   But you remain **shy**.   You are encouraged to take control and be assertive by gaining control of your body language.   You can use repeated affirmations:*

1. **"I will not blink."**
2. **"I will not blush."**

3. **"I will not cry."**
4. **"I will not faint."**

5. **"I will not run."**
6. **"I will not hide."**

7. **"I will not back down."**
8. **"I will not wind down."**

9. **"I will not stoop."**
10. **"I will not stop."**

By repeating aloud these simple positive decisions, you will discover a new presence and personality.   You will find that you can proudly take your rightful place at life's banquet table.
***You can be yourself.** You can be seen and known for who and what you really are.*

–Dr. YES!

10

Going All The Way

("YES! I'll give it a try")

> *To commit is to inherit everything and to persist
> is to claim it for yourself, as much or as
> little as you choose.*
>
> —A.C.S.

The rain was pouring down. Madeleine stood impatiently in the foyer, looking out the window.

She had called for a taxi almost half an hour ago and there was still nothing in sight. Her flight was leaving in just over an hour and on the best of days, it was a good fifteen minutes to the airport. But she could not afford to let herself become stressed. This meeting was too important.

For months this hard working entrepreneur had been trying to nail this particular piece of business, and finally it was within her grasp.

Come on, where was that taxi?

She glanced at her Seiko watch. Time was closing in. She peeked out the window again but all she could see were more sheets of rain pounding the street in front of her house in an intense early spring downpour.

As she waited, she drifted over to the mirror and checked her make-up one last time. She was really quite an attractive woman, but the bright hallway light this morning was unforgiving. It was hard to ignore the creeping shadows under her eyes and the tiny "squint" wrinkles that popped up every time she smiled.

'Well,' she thought to herself, 'not bad for a lady with three teenage children.'

She let out a soft chuckle. 'Not bad at all.'

Ding-dong. Madeleine jumped.

Why had the taxi interrupted her moment of indulgence?

But she soon remembered her mission today. She must not be late.

So she let the driver carry her luggage ahead, then she hustled carefully while holding her small umbrella, out through the rain, down the steps, across the pavement and into the open door of the cab.

As they ploughed through the water on the congested city streets, Madeleine noticed the picture of a young girl on the dashboard.

"Is that your daughter's picture, sir?"

"Yes, ma'am. That's my only child. She's now sixteen and she gave me that picture on her birthday last month. Daddy's girl, you know."

"She's very pretty. You must be proud."

"I wouldn't argue with either comment, ma'am. But everyone says she looks like her mother." He smiled.

"Don't all pretty girls?"

"I only have one, ma'am. No boys." He seemed disappointed.

"I have only three teenage daughters myself."

"Good for you, ma'am. You could have three sons-in-law later." He smirked to himself.

"Let's not talk about that."

Madeleine had good reason to avoid the subject. With that brief conversation, she got a quick reminder of the other important thing in her life. She had lots to think about. In fact, a wave of emotion came over her and she became very pensive and quiet. She tried to focus on her upcoming meeting, but it was no use.

Two nights ago she had had an agonizing and teary scene with her second daughter, Pat. The details kept shoving their way relentlessly into her thoughts. It was a very unpleasant confrontation, largely because it was regarding a very unpleasant issue.

Pat was a seventeen year old honor student at the local high school and she had come home from the doctor's office a week ago to announce to the family that she was six weeks pregnant. She had obviously prepared for the announcement and chose her moment when dad was out of town on business.

Well, that little conversational nugget had certainly chilled down the after-dinner talk.

Madeleine still had not made the mental adjustment to the fact that 'her little baby' was going to have a baby.

The sisters had mixed reactions since they had each seen friends at school become pregnant too, but now it was their own sister, Pat, on the hot seat.

What would dad think when he got back? That was worth betting on.

Two nights ago they had finally had a conversation about where this was all going to lead. It was a mother and child wrestling over the fate of a different mother and a different child.

Madeleine was surprised to learn that her daughter had some real reservations about terminating her pregnancy. Yet she herself was absolutely convinced that it would be ridiculous to do otherwise.

It would change everything. Pat was too young and unprepared for the responsibilities of motherhood. She would be foolish to let her chances of a professional education slip. Getting pregnant was the first mistake but having the baby would be the second. It was not convenient at this time and nothing was going to change that.

It was a case of Hobson's choice, to do the only thing that she could do, given the nature of her circumstances. It was her right to choose. Her body. Her future. Her life. It could be clean, clinical and complication-free. Perhaps a little emotional upset, and then it would be back to business as usual.

At least, Madeleine minimized the implications.

Pat tried to listen to what her mom had to say. She could not hold back the tears. She tried to articulate some of her feelings but her mom remained single-minded.

Yet like a caring mother, Madeleine had been understanding to a point. However, toward the end of the conversation she had to admit that she had said some things that she regretted. She had called Pat immature and selfish, and neither was fair, but it had slipped out in the heat of the battle.

Still, as Madeleine sat in the back of the cab today, her opinion hadn't changed. She was still absolutely sure that the best thing her daughter could do for herself was to terminate her pregnancy and get on with her teenage life. She could finish school normally and be off to college without interruption or distraction. There would be lots of time left for motherhood. Plus, she could save the family from major embarrassment.

The focus was entirely on the future and well-being of Pat and the family. The fetus was an unknown entity of dubious significance, dispensable and disposable if, and only if, the mom chose to declare it so. All else was speculation.

That's how Madeleine thought.

But Pat herself was not so sure. She knew she was carrying a new life within her womb. She felt honored and she felt responsible. It was unplanned but not unwanted. Her emotions were as turbulent as her convictions were tenuous.

She listened to her mom but could not be so quick to terminate her pregnancy. She had not yet come to terms with her options. After all, she could not put out of her mind the thought that in her womb was *'a child, not a choice'*. Could she have the baby, even secretly and perhaps then give it up for adoption? Should she make her choice *after* birth?

The tension at home persisted and yet, time was of the essence.

But Madeleine had to let that go, at least for a little while. This meeting in Denver had to go well, and she had to spend some time thinking about it to make sure that it did.

It did not seem to take as long as Madeleine had feared to get to the airport. As she stepped out of the cab, she paused again to look at the picture on the dashboard and she could feel a tear-drop filling her eyes as she shuddered with nostalgia.

"Give your girl a hug for me, will you?"

She tipped the driver and rushed into the terminal, pulling her roll-on luggage while her handbag swung freely like a pendulum as she moved. She checked the monitors and hurried directly to her gate.

She was somewhat relieved to learn that her plane was delayed. It was late arriving in Seattle and so the departure time would be thirty minutes later. She could at least catch her breath, gather her thoughts and freshen up.

She then took a seat over against the glass wall.

In the common waiting area, a boy, perhaps ten or twelve, and an older man, quite possibly grandson and grandfather, were sitting in front of the gate for Denver, which was adjacent to the gate for St. Louis. The plane for Denver had not yet arrived at the gate.

The man and the boy had a good view of the northern runway. Both of them were dressed casually, and neither seemed to have any luggage. They were probably meeting someone today. They were content to just sit and watch the planes take off and land. The boy had many questions which the man seemed to have no problem answering.

Madeleine sat beside them and was fascinated by the boy's inquisitiveness. She tried to imagine the kinds of questions she would soon be asked in the boardroom.

Here she was, a meeting planner on her way to Denver to see her hottest prospect. It was a company that was planning a big national meeting that would last 5-7 days and require close to 700 sleeping rooms. That would make it by far the biggest account that Madeleine had ever closed.

She was nervous. She desperately wanted the account, but she was afraid that it could slip away.

Her original meetings with the client had gone well, even though she did not have all the answers at that time. But then she had also been slow about following up with a strong proposal. She had sounded far too tentative about how she was going to handle some details of the large meeting.

Lately, the client had been somewhat more distant on the telephone, but she was not eliminated and Madeleine was heading to Denver determined to salvage the account.

She could hear the boy and the old man speaking.

"Grandpa," said the boy, "how fast does that plane fly?"

The old man answered in a soft voice:

"Well, it has a top speed of about 600 miles per hour, which is almost as fast as the speed of sound. It's a heck of a lot faster than you can run, that's for sure."

"All the people went on that plane, Grandpa," the boy observed, as he pointed to the shiny jet at the St. Louis gate.

"Why don't they leave?"

"To start with, they can't leave until the ground crew and the air traffic controllers give the pilot permission. When it's time, they'll get clearance to 'push back'.

"But as they wait, they're very busy. The pilot and co-pilot have to make sure everything is ready. They'll check the instruments, the fuel, the electronics, the weather, the flight plan. And after they are all finished, they check them again.

"At this stage of the flight, abundant caution and careful attention to detail is most important. The pilot has to be very cautious in his preparation."

Madeleine thought about her own preparation for the previous Denver meeting and she realized that her own preparation had been half-hearted. She had skimmed over the research on her client and the proposal had been short on contingencies.

Madeleine crossed her legs and tightened her grip on the handbag she had on her lap. The boy's excitement helped to ease her anxiety.

"It's moving Grandpa, it's moving... "

The big jet was pushing back from the gate and the pilot was following the instructions of the ground crew to steer the jet out on to the runway.

"Notice," the man began, "how much help the pilot gets at this stage of the flight. He is relying on the ground crew and on the air traffic controllers to get into position for take-off. He can't have a successful flight unless he is willing to acknowledge and accept the help."

Madeleine knew it was true. There was an older meeting planner in her small company who had dealt with her prospect eight years ago. In fact, that's how she got the lead in the first place, but Madeleine had brushed off his suggestions as being outdated. She probably could have benefited from his input.

The plane to St. Louis was soon on the runway, and the man and the boy were standing by the window eagerly watching it.

Madeleine got up and stood behind them at a respectful distance, but still close enough to hear the conversation. She wondered if the old man was a retired air force or commercial pilot. He seemed so knowledgeable about airplanes. She wanted to eavesdrop on some more wisdom being dispensed so freely, as if from a heavenly messenger to her. The man was again speaking to the boy:

"Okay Willy, now they are ready to go. They are Number One for take-off. Everything has been carefully checked and the flight crew has relied on the help of all the other people to get the airplane up in the air."

The airplane started to hurtle down the runway picking up speed as it went. Smoke was pouring out the back of the engines but the nose cone seemed to pierce the air with a deliberate determination as if on a mission of destiny. The hard rubber wheels were spitting as if to say 'thanks, but no thanks' for the burden.

"Look Willy, this is important. Once that pilot has started down the runway, there comes a point in time when there is no turning back. That's called a point of no return.

"Once they are speeding down the runway, the time for caution is over. That's it. The time for hesitation is over. The time for second guessing is over. They are committed.

"The only thing that the pilot can do is to pull back, race down that runway at near top speed and aim to get that beautiful bird airborne. There is no turning back. It's all or nothing. You can't go half way. It's all the way ... or forget it. It would be a disaster. You don't get a 100-ton aircraft into the air by half measures."

"Wow, I would like to try something like that. It must be fun and really exciting."

The boy's eyes were tracking the plane as it ascended into the cloud cover leaving a rarefied trail of smoke like graffiti across the sky.

The old man shifted so that he could make direct eye contact with the boy. He seemed intent on communication.

"A schoolboy's try would never be good enough. It's do or die, so you can't just give it a try.

"Willy, I can tell you from experience, I've watched people try and not get what they want for a long time. Many of them fail because they are just going through motions, putting in only half an effort. They pursue their dreams in a half hearted way. It doesn't work.

"This plane is a perfect example. Aircraft flight requires momentum; just like that, success requires momentum. Never expect success when you're just going through the motions. You must decide and then go for it."

Madeleine listened to every word, and she thought about her trip and the lack of confidence she had when she was talking to her client at the last meeting. She remembered the tip toeing around that she did when suggesting activities or possible sites for the conference. She had absolutely no momentum or energy, no enthusiasm--she had been too petrified that she would make a mistake and she had been so cautious and careful that the whole project had just about run out of steam.

Almost.

At that moment she made a decision.

This time she would have to come at the client with all the energy and confidence that she could muster. It might not work; maybe it was too late. But she knew one thing: the overly cautious and timid approach was certainly not going to work. She might as well give it an all-out effort, the best shot she had. She was determined to go all the way, give it everything she knew, win or lose ... who knows ... maybe her ideas would fly.

She followed through.

In Denver, she *appeared* sharp. Her *attitude* was confident, strong and persuasive. She was very *affable* and advanced her ideas and proposals for the upcoming meeting. She was well received and she was most *appreciative* of the recognition she got. She *affirmed* that this upcoming meeting would be the best in the company's history, judging by established diagnostic and evaluation criteria. She won the *affection* of her clients. She scored all A's. There was only one missing piece and that would be resolved over dinner.

Madeleine was elated as she sat in the waiting room of the restaurant that evening. It looked like she had made a good enough presentation and if she kept it up, she was going to get the contract. But she knew it wasn't a done deal, at least not quite yet.

The company vice-president, Bob Wilson, had asked her to have dinner with him and his wife, Dr. Pamela Lewis, at a fashionable restaurant up town. And that could only mean one thing. He wanted to have his wife informally give Madeleine her stamp of approval.

That was fine. She knew she had cleared the big hurdles and she loved to get together with other professional women to share experiences and unwind.

Bob and Pam walked in late, but only by about fifteen minutes and after a brief apology about something at the hospital, they were seated at an excellent table on the mezzanine.

Madeleine warmed up to Pam right away as if they had known each other before.

"Pam, Bob told me you were a doctor, but he didn't say what kind." Madeleine was curious.

"Well, we're all doctors I guess, but I do specialize in obstetrics and gynecology."

"Really? I'm so glad that you ladies are out there ... twenty years ago you could hardly find a woman to go to."

"Yes, the whole profession has changed. But we're so busy we don't get to thinking a lot about that. I guess in your line of work, it's the same thing."

"Not really. For a long time, meeting planners were like moms, looking after a business group just like they would look after their family. And you know, the brain was always taken for granted, just like moms. But mom is everything, all in one; so is planning a meeting. More men should try doing my job. They would find out what most stay-at-home husbands did."

Madeleine and Pam engaged over dinner in a way that was so relaxed and enjoyable. Bob seemed to be just listening as he smoked his pipe after the meal. No mention was made of the conference itself. It was not necessary and Madeleine decided that Pam was much too smooth for that.

In fact, she was a remarkable woman. She was a top specialist in high risk pregnancies but she was also modest and unassuming, and as Madeleine had happily discovered, she had an excellent sense of humor.

They covered all kinds of ground over dinner, from vacation plans to professional challenges, to the best hotels in the Caribbean. All very pleasant. But then Madeleine asked what she thought was a very innocent question.

"What's you favorite part of the job? What do you enjoy most about being a doctor?"

"No question about that," Pam responded immediately. "The reason I became a doctor in the first place, and the reason I became a specialist, was because I just love delivering babies. I must have delivered thousands by now, but I never get over the thrill of bringing a new life into the world. It's even more special if there are complications and everything turns out right in the end. You get to feel like you're saving lives ... and doing so very early. Each one is so special. I'm very fortunate."

The two of them shared stories of childbirth as Madeleine talked about her three children and Pam talked about her two teenagers. Madeleine decided, even though it was supposed to be a business dinner, to ask a question that often puzzled her. Perhaps more so in the past week.

"Can I ask you something, Pam, something that I've often wondered about?"

"Surely ... Please do."

"I've often wondered how obstetricians can handle the two extremes of their job. On the one hand, you deliver babies and get involved in all the excitement and challenge of that. But on the other hand, doctors are also professionally responsible for terminating pregnancies when the mother decides she does not want the child. Does that create any internal tension for you?"

"Well ... I can't speak for my colleagues ... but personally, it doesn't create any tension for me, because I don't perform abortions myself. Never have and never will."

"Oh ... of course ... I never meant to get ..." Madeleine felt very uncomfortable all of a sudden.

"Don't worry. I think it was a good question. I've often wondered the same thing. When I was in medical school, where this question is virtually ignored, I was struck by the same dichotomy. I saw specialists struggle with a difficult delivery in the morning and do D. & C. abortions in the afternoon. I could not understand it.

"After all, when a woman is pregnant, she has something alive in her. There is no doubt that it's alive. Even at six weeks you can discern the developing fetal structures. That is a person in embryo. The whole point of an abortion is to take what is alive and make it unalive. It seems to me that after conception, you pass the point of no return. Left alone, that's a baby unless something else happens. Drugs. Saline. Suction. Curettage. Something active and voluntary is done to destroy that baby in embryo."

Madeleine was crying inside. She stared back at Pam as if she had just been blinded by the light and managed to open her eyes to see again.

'The point of no return ... the point of no return?'

Madeleine echoed the phrase as she remembered the old man and his grandson at the airport. But her mind was obviously fixed on her daughter, Pat.

As for Pam, she was not finished speaking.

"That human fetal tissue is alive, and after the abortion, it is ... dead. I decided after seeing that in Med School, right there and then, that I would never, ever, perform an abortion. I just couldn't. Either *all* human life is invaluable or *no* life is valuable."

Madeleine's expression invited Pat to go on. Bob had heard this all before so he just sat and listened without showing any emotion.

"I realized that nothing magical happens to that infant when it leaves the womb of its mother. Birth doesn't make that baby any more human that it was two hours before it was born. Or two weeks, or two months ... or two trimesters for that matter. There is no such thing as half-a-human. That baby is a baby right from the time it first starts to grow. There is no half way. It is all or nothing. And furthermore, my oath as a doctor is to protect and cherish human life ... not to end it."

There was a deafening silence as the weight of Pam's conviction rested heavily on Madeleine's mind. She seemed to be in a state of shock. She had thought that the issue for Pat was simple. Now she was not sure. Perhaps she had been wrong all along.

"Well ... those are my feelings ... perhaps I'm not politically correct but morally, I feel good ... what about you, Madeleine?"

Madeleine took a big gulp.

She wanted to be neither pro-choice or pro-life. She would now be content to just choose life. Somehow, politics now seemed irrelevant, the question of rights became remote and the issue of convenience appeared redundant.

The light dawned.

"Excuse me ... I have to make a telephone call."

She rushed out to call Pat.

Pat was elated to hear from her mom ... They chatted. More like true dialogue. Both mother and child were now more sensitive to child and grandchild. There was rising anticipation.

"We can handle this ... together."

What a relief that was. One mother and child reunion had just saved another mother and child union.

Madeleine returned to the table in tears. She shared her story about her daughter's pregnancy and the evening ended in a warm and caring session. No wonder, Bob and Pam also had a seventeen year old daughter.

Madeleine got the contract.

Pat got a baby girl ... and named her ... Pam.

What if ...?

*   *   *

GO FOR IT!

There comes a challenge you will find,
A time to leave the past behind.
It is this point of no return:
A time to all those bridges burn.

'Tis fatal to look back to see
What could have been, that'll never be.
When now before you comes the call
To go for broke, to give your all.

You've got to have the attitude
To gain that cruising altitude.
The clouds were never meant to be
A ceiling for eternity.

So pull out all the stops you've got
And go for it. It matters not
What consequences will ensue –
In the real game of life, nothing less will do.

—A.C.S.

The Compliance Test

Recall that this book is a prescription.
Having read this tale, you may experience some "side effects."
*Take some time now to **describe** any of the possible "side effects" that you observe:*

–Dr. YES!

Inspiration ...

Entertainment ...

Challenge ...

Imagination ...

Breakthrough ...

Self-discovery ...

Crisis ...

Motivation ...

Humor ...

Increased appetite for ... YES!

YOUR PRESCRIPTION

TEN (10) GREEN LIGHTS

*You probably responded to the challenge and opportunities of life with some reservation. You said **"YES, I'll give it a try"**. But you now can see a series of green lights up ahead, beckoning you to do much more than that. Each one projects a distinct message:*

1. **Move. Don't stand still.**
2. **Accelerate. Don't cruise.**
3. **Fly. Accept no limitations.**
4. **Commit. Don't hold back.**
5. **Stay Alert. Don't drift.**
6. **Lead. Don't tailgate.**
7. **Let go. Leave the past behind.**
8. **Anticipate. Be proactive.**
9. **Relax. Danger is over.**
10. **Enjoy the Trip.**

*Just the sight of this row of green lights causes your adrenaline to surge. **You are committed.** You've passed the point of no return. This is living with passion and flair. You're almost there.*

–Dr. YES!

11

Best Is Not Enough

("YES!! I'll do my best")

*'Better' is the bridge between good and best,
but it also connects your personal best
with everything else.*

—A.C.S.

Family life is a challenge. Small business is also a big challenge. Combine both of these and a small, family-run business is double jeopardy.

The challenge of family life is to find harmony among different individuals who each have unique backgrounds, distinct personalities, separate interests and styles, and often conflicting values.

With defined roles and clear lines of authority and accountability, most families are strained at the edges because every member is forced to compromise. Strategies of open communication, unselfishness and love, as well as mutual respect and cooperation, all go a long way to overcoming the friction and centrifugal forces that inevitably arise.

The Cunninghams were not perfect but they were a good family. Doug and Donna were baby boomers who had migrated to the city when their kids were very small. They wanted the advantage of urban schools and they were both anxious to leave farm life behind. The girls were now teenagers in grades nine and twelve and had not manifested any extreme behaviors in adolescence. They were good kids. Just as well. The strain of the family business was already testing the relationship between mom and dad.

The challenges of small business come from all sides. Even after entrepreneurs do adequate homework and preparation, there are all types of problems that cannot be anticipated. Small businesses survive in a narrow window between adequate cash flow, favorable market trends, controlled overhead costs, government red tape and burdensome procedures.

Then there's tax policy, interest rates, fierce competition, satisfied customers and much more. It is in most cases a delicate balancing act just to stay in business, especially when the economy is not growing.

The Cunninghams were living in this plight. They were struggling. Doug knew it. Donna knew it. But they both kept the kids in the dark. After seven years, things were truly not going well at their retail picture frame depot.

Doug had been working extended hours for the past few months. He was convinced that when 'the going get tough, the tough must get going'. So he had redoubled his efforts.

With his strong Dutch Mennonite heritage he had an exaggerated work ethic. He took personal responsibility for the business, since it was his idea from the start, and he considered his wife a helper. In his mind, she did not need to know everything about the business. That was his job.

He was prepared to do whatever it would take to make a 'go' of the venture. He believed success would be his reward for hard work. So he worked harder and harder still.

But he had his limitations. He could not do it all. He could not be in different places meeting different needs of the business at the same time.

On this particular Monday evening, he had gone across town to meet with a new supplier. That left Donna with a couple of free hours to poke around, especially since the customer traffic was very light.

The store sold frames and pictures, as well as some art supplies. There was one lone customer in the store that evening, browsing through the black and white prints. The place was well kept and always looked bright and inviting. The selection was good and Doug kept the inventory fresh and dusted. The mall they were in had good traffic and in fact, the store itself usually had many browsers. But not many of them purchased anything.

Recently Doug had set up a self-serve table for people who wanted to do their own framing. He figured do-it-yourself framing would be a good way to get more people into the store. Once inside, the customers would have more time to interact with the owners. This would create the opportunity to cross-sell the other items that they carried. It would also be more interesting.

That all looked like a good idea. Even Donna had agreed.

From the start, the change did increase the number of people coming into the store. But Doug overlooked a key point: people who do their own framing, do it to save money. So they weren't much interested in buying other items that the store carried.

The self-serve table had been operating for about a year, but it was still hard for Doug to determine whether it really was making money.

Donna had no way to tell if anything was making money. She did none of the purchasing and none of the business banking.

Maybe today she could find out something new. She was on a mission but she had to be quick and careful.

She opened the cabinet under the cash register. There were ledgers with daily sales entries. She tried to make some sense of the numbers but could not understand the different columns of figures.

Doug had been very reluctant to share daily sales numbers with her when she asked. She would have loved to see for herself how much product they were really moving.

There was no distrust or suspicion on her part. After all, she and Doug were married eighteen years ago, and for most of the marriage they had enjoyed free and open communication.

When Doug quit his job at the hydro plant he had changed the rules. He would be the Minister of Industry and Finance, while Donna would be the Minister of Home Affairs. He would help her with her duties and likewise, she would help in the business. But only in the service area, not in management, in either case. For the past seven years, the struggles of the business had intensified. Now Donna wanted them to get out. She wanted to sell the store to whoever would buy it. She had concluded that if you couldn't make it in retail after seven years of long hours and meager pay, then inevitably you couldn't make it at all.

Doug was apparently spinning his wheels and Donna wanted to put the brakes on.

She kept searching for something. She knew not what. On the top shelf of the cabinet she found some old cash register tapes in a small cardboard box.

Donna looked at some numbers she could now understand. Over the last two months, she had learned how to figure out the total revenue as entered on the store register. She reverted to her school arithmetic and for the next while she was busy doing addition and subtraction.

She did know what the rent was and how much Doug was drawing for their services in the store. That was enough for her. She did not need to be a rocket scientist to figure out that the store was operating in the gray zone.

She really was not surprised. Her fears were now confirmed. At best, the store was not making money.

Only if Doug cut his wages in half, and managed to set up a credit account with any proposed new supplier, could he keep the store open. And no doubt if she pressed, that was exactly what Doug was intending to do.

Donna realized the plain truth--they had no idea why sales were so low.

Looking back, she asked herself what she had learned about the retail business over the last five years. Certainly in the beginning there was lots to learn, but over the last two years they were still trying the same things that had failed five years ago. There had been no growth at all, and after seven years in the business, that was inexcusable.

Donna figured that if they stayed in business, five years from now they would still be trying the same things, because they didn't know what else to do.

It had taken her seven years to figure it out, but she had finally decided that you either grow or die, and when it came to the picture frame business, they were dying. Growth had been negligible.

Donna walked over to the empty self-serve table and sat on one of the stools. She looked around the store. Everywhere she looked she could see glimpses of her Doug.

She had to admit that he had put in long hours and worked incredibly hard, trying to come up with a formula that was successful. He was giving it everything he had. It was that fact more than anything else that had kept Donna quiet for so long. But time was running out. Should she call the score?

Donna was determined that she wasn't going to spend the next twenty years as the living dead, so she pulled out the telephone book. She flipped it open and turned to the listing for business brokers. She was feeling an ominous excitement mingled with more nervous apprehension.

"Why not try and get a broker to put a value on the business and then see what it would take to get it listed?"

Donna decided she would be proactive. Then when Doug came around, everything would be in place.

She picked up the telephone and placed the call.

The phone had only rung twice when Donna had a sudden change of mind and she hung up.

She knew that taking control was definitely not the way to deal with Doug. He would be furious.

After all, life only called for three simple arts: passion, balance and diplomacy. Doug seemed to have a lot of the first, while she took pride in the second. She realized that she had just then mastered the third. She would have to work on Doug with deference and sensitivity.

The next morning after breakfast, the girls had left for

school and Donna had a chance to talk to Doug about her feelings, about what she had wanted to do with the store.

The conversation was tense. Over the third cup of coffee, Donna continued to say her piece.

"You've done everything there is to do, Doug. The store is just not working. It's not your fault, but we have to be realistic. We have to think about moving on."

Doug appeared to be studying the back of the cereal box on the table with great interest. He did not look up.

"Just be patient, Donna. Give it a little more time."

"We've put seven years into the business, Doug, and we don't have anything to show for it. There comes a point in time when you have to cut your losses. I think that time has come."

Donna was direct but in caring, sensitive tones. She knew this was not an easy confrontation for Doug to handle, either way. Was he listening? Was he getting angry?

Doug finally looked at Donna:

"I need support, Donna, not mutiny. Listen ... I'm doing my best. I'm busting my butt trying to turn the situation around. Things have to turn around, eventually. They'll turn around a lot quicker if you're behind me, instead of fighting me."

Donna paused and let the air fill up with silence. Then very slowly, and in the most level and centered tone she could summon, she tried to continue the dialogue.

"Doug, I know you've done your best. I know the kind of hours you've put in. I know that you've tried everything you can think of. I know you've done all that you know to do. But Doug ... what happens when your best ... your very best ... is just not good enough? Have you ever asked that question? The fact that you've done your best is the reason why we should think about moving on. Your best ... my best ... have just not been good enough. We have to face that music."

Donna fiddled with the slices of apple left on her breakfast plate. Doug was looking at her intently, but he didn't say a word. She pressed on.

"Doug, what if things don't eventually turn around? I think you're stuck ... or maybe we're both stuck ... in some kind of magical thinking. We think that life is like a Morality Play where the good guys always triumph in the end. We think that if we work hard, try our best, put in the hours, then in the long run, somewhere, somehow, we're going to succeed in this business. I'm probably just as guilty as you are."

The change in Doug's countenance was the first sign that he had heard something. At least, now she knew he was listening. Donna felt encouraged to continue. Softly.

"But Doug ... life is not a Morality Play. The good guys don't always win in the end. The seven years we have put into this business could even double or triple and we could still be no further ahead."

She paused and even waited for a while to let that warning shot lodge in Doug's brain. Then she fired again.

"Success in business she continued," is not simply about trying hard. It is about winning. Businesses exist to make a profit. I'm sure you would agree with that. It's elementary. Big business can sometimes absorb losses but just think of us. Can we, much longer?"

Again, Donna let the truth sink in. She could tell she was making some impression. What kind? She was not at all sure.

"We haven't been able to grow the business. We can't simply continue on, mindlessly marching to the same tune with the proviso in the back of our minds that 'eventually things will get better'. I think it's time that we got honest with ourselves and admit that when it comes to selling picture frames, our best is just not good enough."

Donna looked to Doug for verbal response but he was getting up from the table. Doug picked up the newspaper from the counter and glanced at the headlines. Then he turned to Donna:

"I'm late for a meeting."

With that he was out the door.

They did not bring up the subject again for the next week.

Finally, the following Friday after supper, young Diane was eager to share her new class project. Her Grade

XII teacher had given a new class assignment with several electives for an independent project. Diane had decided all by herself to write a paper on "Running a Small Business". She knew she had an advantage with that one. She was eager to get going and thought her best starting point was to interview her own successful entrepreneurial parents who had done such a super job over the past few years right before her eyes.

She obviously had never seen the books or the bills.

"That's a great idea," Mom was delighted to point out.

"I think that is a major challenge." Doug smiled.

Dad was not really enthused. He felt vulnerable and already began to fear the worst. But he only had one choice. He thought for a moment and decided to go on the offensive.

"In fact, here's what I suggest, Diane. You will be biased if you begin with us and I'm sure you already know that the mark of good academic work is a high degree of objectivity. You want to have no preconceived notions, no clear preferences for anything you find. It's really hard to keep emotion out of a family study ... your own family. So what I suggest is this. Begin with some objective sources, and ..."

Diane jumped in.

"I've already been thinking about that. I'm going to see the Business teacher at the vocational college on the East side. I have his name and number in my satchel. Then I plan to talk to six business owners in the same mall as our Depot and then three other art shop owners in the city. Then I will spend some time in the library reading and researching small business magazines to complete my background work."

"We have not seen a business magazine in years. Maybe you could purchase a couple of recent issues and work with those at home."   Donna perked up.

Mom had her own intentions in mind.   Diane continued:

"But sooner or later I'll have to talk with both of you to get some more personal data to make a thorough thesis. A good piece of academic work should also be exhaustive, sparing no punches. There must be an upside and a downside to any business.   There's always what goes on behind the scenes that no one else knows.   Who better to learn all this from than my own successful parents?"

"Agreed."   Doug closed the loop.

Dad wanted to appear cooperative, for his daughters were both very close and dear to him. That's perhaps why he was trying so hard at his business in the first place.

"Sounds good to me.   But what should I know? ... When will you get started?" Diane's baby sister wanted to get practical.   "Can't I do something too?"

"Sure you can, Danielle.   I was thinking, since you like to take pictures so much, you could be responsible for illustrating the project. You can use dad's camera and take as many pictures as you want at the mall. Of course you will take lots inside and outside our Depot, won't you?"

Everybody seemed delighted. It had become a family affair for now, at least.

One month later, they were all bursting with new ideas. Diane had discovered that many of the challenges of small business could be addressed by focusing on three key areas: containing overhead costs, effective advertising and promotions to increase revenues, and above all, customer satisfaction to build loyalty and a growing referral base. She focused her paper on these three areas.

The whole family was in on the supper discussions night after night. They shared ideas.

Three months later, her parents could not believe what was happening. They themselves were treating their customers differently. They were talking to suppliers about creative promotions at minimal expense. They were attracting attention in the mall with features like dressing the girls in costumes to hand out balloons outside the store.

They had an in-store raffle of a feature print that was on display in the mall. Suppliers representatives were visiting and spending time in the store, answering customers questions.

They put gift coupons in welcome wagon packets for the young parents in the growing communities on the East side. They bought new soccer jerseys for Danielle's junior league team that went all the way to the finals.

They had a promotional article in the city paper which explained all the features and benefits of do-it-yourself framing including one of Danielle's own pictures as a special highlight.

They bought a coffee-maker at a garage sale and served complimentary coffee to the patrons. They added a jar for donations in support of the local association for the visually challenged.

They renegotiated their lease in the mall with huge savings and cancelled their computer contract.

They had to hire two new employees just to service the flood of new customers.

Yes! They were in business!

The bottom line was that Diane got an 'A' for her Assignment. Doug got a 'B' for his new profitable Business. They all got a 'C' for a new Cunningham family.

And why all this success?

Because Doug's best got much better. He could have remained a 'D' --heading for imminent Disaster, despite his best intentions. But the family pulled off an 'E' together. They found their breakthrough by striving for Excellence.

What do *you* do when your best is still not good enough?

*   *   *

THE MARK

Brethren,
I count not myself
to have apprehended.

But this one thing I do:
forgetting those things
which are behind,
And reaching forth
unto those things
which are before,

I press
toward the mark
for the prize
of my high calling ...

—St. Paul

The Compliance Test

Recall that this book is a prescription.
Having read this tale, you may experience some "side effects."
*Take some time now to **describe** any of the possible "side effects" that you observe:*
–Dr. YES!

Inspiration ...

Entertainment ...

Challenge ...

Imagination ...

Breakthrough ...

Self-discovery ...

Crisis ...

Motivation ...

Humor ...

Increased appetite for ... YES!

YOUR PRESCRIPTION

TEN (10) ROOTS TO GROWTH

*When you have **done your best** and your proven best is not good enough, you must always seek to get better. You can draw from the roots that are nourished by life's enduring values. How?*

1. **Learn from your mistakes.**
2. **Take a vacation.**
3. **Travel.**
4. **Read Widely.**
5. **Cherish your family.**
6. **Discipline yourself.**
7. **Serve.**
8. **Stand for principle.**
9. **Revise your purpose.**
10. **Meditate.**

*As you continue to feed on the inflow from these practical life channels, you will indeed **get better** and you will keep growing towards the stars of your greater destiny. Forever.*

–Dr. YES!

PREAMBLE to YES!!!

Evolutionary Tales is a prescription for you.

You are the patient - with or without symptoms! So, how then fares the patient?... Improved?... Improving?

Did you complete the Compliance Tests? Were there side effects that you observed?

Have you now personally found that 'in each Tale, there's always *more than just a tale*'?

Did you find yourself reflected somewhere along the continuum?

Was there an obvious progression as you discerned those **Evolutionary Tales**?

Can you identify with the imminent consummation?

If you answered **YES!** to all those questions, then read on. The following affirmation and challenge is yours.

If you still have residual barriers to truly affirmative living, then you may need to re-read one or more specific Tales. Otherwise, you may choose to go directly on to the other books in *The* **YES!** *Trilogy:*

Part 1, **Your Evolution to YES!**

or

Part 2, **Understanding the Evolution of YES!**

Sooner or later, if not now, you will relate to the consummate stage which follows immediately. You will then have something to celebrate.

Celebrate **YES!** *Consummate* **YES!**

12

YES!!!

("YES!!! I'll do it even if it kills me")

Congratulations!

You have now completed *The Evolution of* **YES!** and indeed, your life has become an exclamation of **YES!**

Let's briefly review the twelve Phases that you have mastered along the journey. They are more cumulative than sequential since none is truly left behind. You will continue to grow in each of these dimensions all the time, for you can always get better. But you can take pride even now in what you have already achieved.

You have discovered who you are and what you are all about in this world. You know you can have, you can do and you can be whatever you choose, now that you have set your mind to it. You refuse to stand on the sidelines anymore, for you are now constrained from within by a true sense of vocation. You can do no less.

There are no conditional qualifications in your

response to life either, for you will take the calculated risk. You will consider all the alternatives available, weigh your real options and then go for it. While others only wish and hope for something better, you have focused the power of your imagination to design the life you choose and all excuses have been cheerfully set aside.

Today your sense of urgency obscures tomorrow, so you cherish the present moment and you will therefore act now. That you will do, not with ambivalence or duplicity, but decisively and resolutely. You now know that it is your inalienable right to pursue your dream and to experience success. And *that* you have defined in your own terms. So you are prepared to ask, to seek and to knock on every door of opportunity at your disposal.

You say **YES!** without the hesitation and trepidation of the proverbial schoolboy's try. You are committed, with no reservations whatsoever, and even when your best efforts prove inadequate, you will continue to grow and to get better. In a word, you will pursue your goals with a reckless abandon as if everything depended on them. You will spare no quarter in the passionate pursuit of excellence.

To that end you will consistently

Think **YES!**
Say **YES!**
and *Live* **YES!**

THINK YES!

Your secret weapon is in your mind for there you have taken control. You refuse to succumb to the pattern of negative influences in the environment. You neglect or reject all such negative ideas and information, from whatever source and no matter how popular they may be. Instead, you choose to focus on the positive aspects of every situation and to maintain an optimistic expectation for the future.

Like Norman Vincent Peale has written, *The Power of **Positive Thinking*** has been released within you as an explosive force for change and achievement. As you consciously elect to think **YES!** you find a new perspective on your circumstances. You have come to believe--to believe in yourself, your future, your world, and perhaps your Maker. All skepticism and cynicism have followed negativism through the door and now you have the sweet comfort of assurance.

There is a buoyancy and an energy that gives you confidence and resilience as you face the challenges ahead. When you think **YES!** you can remain calm in the midst of turbulence and uncertainty. You feel stronger than ever and you will move forward with conviction and purposefulness. You are empowered to influence others and to make a real difference in your world.

But your thoughts go beyond just attitude and assurance. They generate activity. Like Robert Schueller has written, you can now *Move Ahead With* **Possibility Thinking**. Between your ears, resides the greatest generator of power in the world. From that seat of consciousness, reason and imagination you can order your new reality into being. It is a power akin to the Divine, to create something out of nothing. It begins with seeing or conceiving that possibility in the mind.

So you now cultivate dreams that surpass all previous experience. When you think **YES!** you crystallize goals that electrify you and draw unexpected streams of blessing into your life. And you carve solutions to problems and difficulties because you are focused sharply on the myriad of possibilities at any given moment.

Your thinking has obviously matured after reading through this book. So you are now invited to go beyond *positive* thinking, and even beyond *possibility* thinking, to discover on an elevated plane, that there is something more:

The Pride of **Positional Thinking**.

To think YES! is
> **to adopt a certain position,**
> **to defend some core principles and**
> **to find for yourself a clear purpose.**

Positional Thinking *is therefore to take a stand for a pattern of life and behavior that makes you remain* *unmoveable, always abounding in **the** work that you now love to do. You have locked in on what is important and your mind-set anchors you to that ground.*

Your conviction is passionate. Your position is clear and firm. Your commitment is unconditional. You know exactly where you stand. You therefore stand tall.

Whatever your circumstance may be just now, and no matter what the challenge you fear or the opportunity you face, you have carved out a position in your mind, that gives you the elusive anchor of both security and serenity. That is the affirmative posture you take. It is the personal resolution that you make. You are constrained by your principles and your sense of purpose. It is your right to live. It is your life to choose ... **YES!**

*From that base you can leverage all your imaginative powers to see beyond your immediate horizons. You can generate solutions. You can create change. You can continue to grow. That is **Positional Thinking.***

From that vantage point you can now *say* **YES!**

SAY YES!

You understand the power of words. In them lies the power of life and death.

Words of encouragement and hope enable the weak and faint to carry on when everything says 'give up and die'.

Words of heroism make young men and women run bravely into bullets.

Spoken in season, kind words build bridges across the chasms of human misunderstanding to touch the heart. But out of season, harsh words tear the most intimate relationships apart.

Gentle words can bring comfort in times of deepest pain and despair, while insensitive words cause wounds, too deep for any echoes to appear.

It is not the quantity of words that constitute their magic and power, it is their quality. It is the form and content that conveys their meaning and empowers them like guided missiles to release incredible power when they strike their intended target. Therefore they are to be launched with care.

Words are often self-fulfilling prophecies. The things you say either empower you or disarm you in the struggle of life. You are never the same on the other side of conscious confession. Each utterance is a contribution to the unfolding reality of your own world and runs a fiber as it were, in the tapestry of your own life. And it is irreversible. Of the 'three things that come not back', the unknown author noted first *'the spoken word,'* then was added 'the sped arrow and the neglected opportunity.'

In *Genesis*, the book of beginnings, all of creation is described in language that suggests there is fundamental value and power in self-expression. There it is written, time and time again, "And God said... and it was so". It is as if in the very *word* of God, resides the very *power* of God.

If that were not enough, in the gospel of *John*, the book of new beginnings, the language is reminiscent and the Greek word '*Logos*' is used to refer to the transcendent Son. He is the eternal living *Word*, the divine effulgence, not unlike the spoken word. But He is distinguished when He "became flesh, and dwelt among us".

And grasp this, "the *Word* of the Lord abides forever". The living Word and the spoken word.

It is not surprising that of all creation, the attribute of verbal communication is given only to *homo sapiens*. Humans alone reflect the essence of that divine image in qualities of self consciousness, reason and verbal communication. We alone are charged to take dominion and to actively participate in the on-going unfolding of creation.

What a privilege!

By our words we can, in part, effect our part. We can both create change and order the direction of that change. We are invited not only to speak to the Throne of Grace above, but also to address the *mountains* that stand in our way below, as well as to confess the *faults* that dog our path, and so to progress beyond them both.

Oh, what power in our words!

The life of **YES!** implies more than thinking. It

involves speaking. Words constitute both the process and the product of such a positive, passionate and productive experience.

May I invite you to do something more. Go back through *The Evolution of YES!* and extract all the useful affirmations that you can use for active confession. Say them aloud and repeat them as often as you need, to generate the internal dynamic of such self-fulfilling expressions. Begin with those words if you choose, and add to them, but use your *choice words* as a source of inspiration and an agent for change in your own life.

As you consistently reiterate words of affirmation, these simple creations of the brain will traverse the all important eighteen inches to the heart. There they will connect with passion, desire and commitment to become explosive forms of human energy that can transform your world. They become more than words or even ideas. They will become mountains of inner strength and resilience that will allow you to face all the challenges of life. They will allow you to see and to seize opportunity as never before. You will therefore grow by leaps and bounds.

That is the transforming magic of affirmation. Try it!

As you continue to grow, be careful of your own words. Accentuate the positive and eliminate the negative. Affirm others just as you affirm yourself.

Keep saying **YES!**

In the face of challenge, you must affirm 'Yes, I can'. In the face of opportunity, again you must affirm 'Yes, I will'. Let there be no 'if's', no 'and's', no 'but's' ... just an unadulterated '**YES!**' It is your life to *confess* ... **YES!**

In every response, look for and choose the preamble, the position or the prospect that leads you to say **YES!** You will find a big difference. You will make an even bigger difference.

When you think about it, that's the only exciting way to live ... to *live* **YES!**

LIVE YES!

Way back there in Phase One, we observed that there is a renewed emphasis today on the term 'quality of life' and all that it implies. The concern is not just as it relates to the senior citizens, as we follow the age wave sweeping in time across the culture. Nor is it just for the terminally ill, now that modern medicine has managed to sustain and prolong the last phase of life to sometimes ridiculous extremes.

But even for the active baby-boomers and those who follow in their wake, this is a time of much social upheaval. Major changes are occurring in the home and in the workplace. Families are being challenged on every front. Everyone seems busier than ever. New technologies are changing our daily routines and responsibilities so that nothing can be taken for granted, including even where, when and how we choose to live and work. No wonder then that many fundamental questions about quality of life have resurfaced.

Some analysts have tried to measure the consequences of this modern change in terms of variables such as leisure, security, income shifts, and the like. These all tend to be 'bread and butter' issues. But life is more than 'bread and butter'. To live **YES!** is to go far beyond the basic necessities of life.

For anyone who must still be concerned with subsistence on a daily basis, they would do well to go back and study *The Evolution of YES!* again. They should find their foothold to spring up and climb out of such circumstance. There is too much bounty and opportunity in the world (at least in *your* world, if you have the privilege of reading this book) to continue a life of just making ends meet.

In the face of free enterprise and with the time, hopefully the health, and the skill-set that you must have, the ideas contained in this book are enough to spur you into action and to cause even the 'down and out' to move up and be included among the 'up and in' crowd. You too can come to think **YES!** to say **YES!** and to live **YES!**

Now, for those readers who dare to consider the life of **YES!**, you will perceive that it is a progressive growth experience in the *Hierarchy of Why.* You first go beyond subsistence, then you move from the social constraints of pride, social acceptance and dignity, to the more personal values of freedom, fulfillment and self-actualization.

Ultimately, the life of **YES!** affirms a strong sense of purpose. You should come to find your place in the world, like the reason and meaning for your existence, and you could take delight in expressing it to the fullest. You would therefore live a life that is resolute and confident.

To live **YES!** is to choose on a daily basis to squeeze from every moment of time, the last drop of possibility. It is to harness all personal resources to advantage and to develop a keen sense of vocation and destiny. That must include giving as much as receiving. You will go beyond mere self interest to seek to make a difference in your world. You will therefore find a spontaneous desire to make each day significant and to pursue excellence without compromise. You want to win but not at all cost. You value playing at the game of life even more than you enjoy attaining the prize. So you engage with reckless abandon.

There is no stopping you now.

You are assured of your own space and so you can make room for all others. This makes for mutual respect and healthy relationships around you. You are now no longer surprised by the generosity of others.

You get back what you give out.

But you are never coy and self-satisfied. You feel like you have only just begun. You welcome each day with eager anticipation for what you are becoming and the opportunity and challenge it affords you to grow, to give and to serve.

To live **YES!** is therefore to live on tip-toe, with your eyes peering over the horizon and your arms outstretched to embrace this moment. Your mind will be at peace but you will be imagining what could yet be, as your heart remains wide open to the world.

This is a life of passion and excitement, a life of vision with integrity. There is no simpler way to put it... it is the life of **YES!** It is your life to *confirm* ... **YES!**

Just live it.

Think **YES!!**

Say   **YES!!**

Live   **YES!!**

–Dr. YES!

The Evolution of **YES!**

You must risk participation
as you pursue your dream,
without excuse now,
by making a clear decision
to be bold enough
and commit to becoming
one who lives with abandon
the exclamation of

YES!!!

In the *now* ...

and in the *end* ...

YES!!!

ORDER FORM

Please rush me the following books:

	Quantity		Each	
☐	GE-10 _____	The "YES!" Trilogy (3 books) @	$54.95	_____
☐	GE-12 _____	Your Evolution to **YES!**	$23.95	_____
☐	GE-13 _____	Understanding the Evolution of **YES!**	$19.95	_____
☐	GE-14 _____	Evolutionary Tales from **Dr. YES!**	$16.95	_____
☐	GE-5 _____	A Passion For Living	$ 4.99	_____

Total Amount of Order $ _____

Telephone orders: Call Toll Free: 1(800) 501-8516

Postal Orders: GOLDENeight Associates
3080 Spring Hill Pkwy, Suite: D
Smyrna, GA 30080

Fax Orders: 1-770-801-0304

☐   Please send the above books to:

Company name: _____

Name: _____

Address: _____ Suite No. _____

City _____ State _____

Zip: _____ - _____ Telephone: (_____) _____

Sales tax:
Georgia residents add pertinent sales tax.

Shipping/Handling:
"The **YES!** *Trilogy"* $6.95 each set. All other books add $2.50 per book.

Payment:
☐   Visa   ☐ Mastercard   Name on card: _____
        Card #: _____ Expiry Date _____
☐   Money order/Certified Check Enclosed
☐   Check

Call toll free **and order NOW.**

NOTES

ORDER FORM - Canadian Residents

Please rush me the following books:

		Quantity		*Each*	
☐	GE-10	_____	The "YES!" Trilogy (3 books) @	$58.95	_____
☐	GE-12	_____	Your Evolution to **YES!**	$26.95	_____
☐	GE-13	_____	Understanding the Evolution of **YES!**	$21.95	_____
☐	GE-14	_____	Evolutionary Tales from **Dr. YES!**	$18.95	_____
☐	GE-5	_____	A Passion For Living	$ 6.99	_____

Total Amount of Order $ _____

Telephone orders: Call Toll Free: 1(800) 501-8516

Postal Orders: GOLDENeight Associates
                            2778 Hargrove Road, Suite: 206
                            Smyrna, GA 30080

Fax Orders: 1-770-801-0304

❏   Please send the above books to:

Company name:_____

Name:_____

Address:_____ Suite No._____

City_____ State_____

Postal Code: _____ Telephone: (_____)_____

Add Sales tax (GST/PST):

Shipping/Handling:
"The **YES!** *Trilogy"* $6.95 each set. All other books add $2.50 per book.

Payment:
❏   Visa   ❏ Mastercard   Name on card:_____
      Card #:_____ Expiry Date_____
❏   Money order/Certified Check Enclosed
❏   Check

Call toll free and order NOW.

NOTES

NOTES

NOTES

NOTES

NOTES

NOTES

NOTES